S0-BZL-998

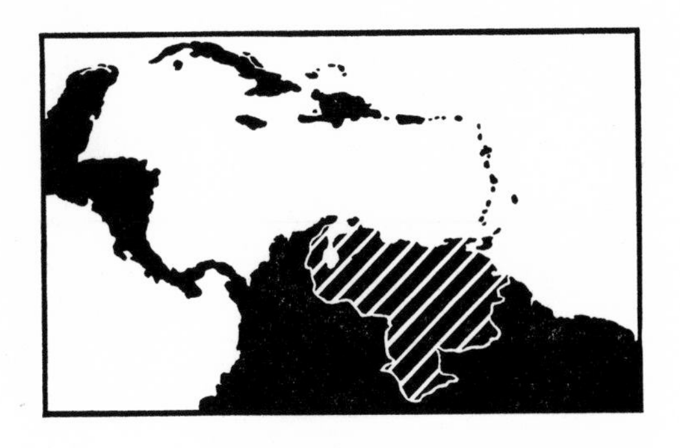

Caribbean Series, 6

Sidney W. Mintz, Editor

PREVIOUS VOLUMES IN THE CARIBBEAN SERIES:

1. *Free Jamaica, 1838–1865: An Economic History*
   By Douglas Hall, 1959

2. *Worker in the Cane: A Puerto Rican Life History*
   By Sidney W. Mintz, 1960

3. *Employment in an Underdeveloped Area: A Sample Survey of Kingston, Jamaica*
   By W. F. Maunder, 1960

4. *Guatemala: The Land and the People*
   By Nathan L. Whetten, 1961

5. *Kinship and Community in Carriacou*
   By M. G. Smith, 1962

Frontispiece. Clay figurine of the Valencia style.

VENEZUELAN ARCHAEOLOGY

by Irving Rouse and José M. Cruxent

YALE UNIVERSITY PRESS, NEW HAVEN AND LONDON, 1963

Designed by Wayne Peterson,
set in Baskerville type,
and printed in the United States of America by
Vail-Ballou Press, Inc., Binghamton, N.Y.

Library of Congress catalog card number: 63-13972

TO ALFREDO BOULTON
Academia de la Historia de Venezuela

AND EDWARD S. DEEVEY AND MINZE STUIVER
Geochronometric Laboratory, Yale University

in appreciation for their assistance
in the work of this volume

PREFACE

This volume is the result of sixteen years' collaboration by its authors in the study of Venezuelan archaeology under the joint sponsorship of Yale University, the Yale Peabody Museum, the Universidad Central de Venezuela, the Museo de Ciencias Naturales, and, most recently, the Instituto Venezolano de Investigaciones Científicas (I.V.I.C.). The Pan American Union has published a technical report of our work for the use of our professional colleagues under the title *An Archeological Chronology of Venezuela* (Cruxent and Rouse, 1958–59, 1961). We attempt here to present the results in a simpler form for the benefit of the non-specialist and the layman interested in Venezuelan archaeology.

In so doing, we have omitted most of the detail and many of the differences in interpretation which the specialist needs to know. We have also kept the bibliography short, including only representative studies of detail and works which, like the present one, are designed to serve as an introduction or survey of the subject.

We have, however, made an exception of the most recent work, done since the completion of our technical report in 1957, including the research which we have jointly carried out in Venezuela during the past two summers. It has seemed advisable to present the results of this research in somewhat more detail, so that the book may also serve as a progress report.

The book has one other purpose. It has been our experience that Venezuelan archaeology is poorly covered, if at all, in general works on the antiquities and aboriginal art of the New World. We have included a relatively large number of plates in an attempt to show that Venezuela has produced artifacts worthy of more general attention than has hitherto been given them.

We wish to take this opportunity to thank all those who have supported or assisted us, including the institutions mentioned above; the Wenner-Gren Foundation for Anthropological Research, Inc., which has awarded grants to both of us; the National Science Foundation, which has supported Rouse's current trip to Venezuela; and the Guggenheim Foundation, from which Cruxent obtained a fellowship to continue his Paleo-Indian studies in the United States. We are likewise indebted to the Geochronometric Laboratory of Yale University and to its Directors, Edward S. Deevey and Minze Stuiver, for analyzing most of our radiocarbon samples. We are especially grateful to Alfredo Boulton and Béla Sziklay for making most of the photographs reproduced in this volume and to Mrs. Shirley Hartman and Sra. Dragoslava de Díaz for their drawings. The other individuals who have aided us are too numerous to mention here; their names may be found in our technical monograph.

Irving Rouse
José M. Cruxent

Caracas, Venezuela
June 1962

CONTENTS

ILLUSTRATIONS

Text Figures

Tables

Chapter 1

INTRODUCTION

A. ORIGIN AND DEVELOPMENT OF THE AMERICAN INDIAN

It is generally agreed that the American Indian entered the New World from Asia. He crossed the Bering Strait into Alaska some time during the last ice age, when the sea stood at a lower level than today and the strait was probably dry. Proceeding eastward into Canada, he is thought to have turned down into the great plains of central North America and passed through a gap in the ice sheets which covered most of Canada at the time. He then spread throughout the United States, continued into Mexico and Central America, and finally expanded into South America.

While it is possible that these events began as early as 40,000 B.C., we know nothing certain about them until the so-called Paleo-Indian epoch, about 15,000 to 5000 B.C. In this epoch, the Indians seem to have lived primarily in the interior of North and South America, where they subsisted by hunting the abundant large land mammals, such as the mammoth, the horse, and the camel, which have since become extinct. "Kill sites," where these animals were butchered, are characteristic. The principal implements consist of chipped stone projectile points which were undoubtedly attached to a wooden shaft and used with a spear thrower. The Paleo-Indians sometimes inhabited caves but more commonly made camps on the open plains where they hunted (Wormington, 1957).

About 8000 B.C. the Indians began to modify their culture in response to the warming of the climate which followed the end of the ice ages. They continued to emphasize the hunting of large land mammals only in the regions most favorable for this activity, such as the plains of the central United States and of Argentina. Elsewhere, they began to rely more upon other means of subsistence, such as fishing along shores and rivers, the gathering of wild vegetable foods in the interior, and, ultimately, the beginnings of agriculture. We may refer to the time of these developments, lasting roughly from 5000 to 1000 B.C., as the Meso-Indian epoch.

Remains of this epoch are easiest to find on islands—including the Antilles, which were first settled at the time—along sea shores and on the banks of rivers, where the Meso-Indians have left remnants of their food in "middens," consisting of piles of shells and fish bones. These middens also contain hearths and, occasionally, burials. Middens are not found away from the water, where we must search for hearths alone, accompanied by scattered deposits of implements and animal bones, in caves or in the open. There is a greater variety of implements than in the Paleo-Indian deposits, including ground as well as chipped stone tools. Mortars or milling stones are the most typical; they were used at first for wild vegetable foods and later to prepare cultivated plants. Clay pottery likewise makes its appearance in the latest Meso-Indian sites of Central America and western South America but was otherwise lacking (Rouse, 1960).

Both the Paleo-Indian and the Meso-Indian ways of life survived in the more remote parts of America until the arrival of Europeans, but throughout most of the Americas the Indians entered a new epoch, the Neo-Indian, about 1000 B.C., which continued until the arrival of Europeans put an end to it around A.D. 1500. Agriculture now became the basic means of subsistence, whereas it had previously been so inefficient that it contributed relatively little to the diet. Increased efficiency made it possible for a larger, more sedentary population to live in villages composed of more permanent houses. In Mexico and Peru, these villages eventually grew into large towns and then into cities, which served as the administrative, commercial, and religious centers for kingdoms and even empires, but elsewhere the Neo-Indians did not attain such a civilized state. Everywhere, however, the increased efficiency of agriculture permitted more leisure time for the development of art and religion. Mexico, in particular, achieved great proficiency in writing, astronomy, and mathematics, while the Peruvian Indians and their neighbors became so adept at metallurgy and weaving that they surpassed their contemporaries of the Old World in certain respects (Braidwood and others, 1962).

The remains of the Neo-Indian period are rich and varied. They include not only food debris, hearths, and burials, but also dwellings and religious structures, sometimes raised on mounds or pyramids. Pottery becomes ubiquitous, except among the Paleo-Indian and Meso-Indian survivors; and other materials such as bone, shell, cotton, and even metals are more widely used for making artifacts. The inventory of artifacts, which had previously been largely utilitarian, now includes many kinds of ceremonial and "problematic" objects, as well as ornaments, frequently found in graves.

In discussing Venezuelan archaeology, we shall also have occasion to refer to an Indo-Hispanic epoch, since the local Indians have survived in some numbers from the time of the arrival of the Spaniards (ca. A.D. 1500) up to the present. The sites of this epoch that have been investigated include not only Indian villages but also missions and other Spanish settlements in which Indian artifacts occur.

B. PLACE OF VENEZUELA IN AMERICAN PREHISTORY

The Paleo- and Meso-Indian remains in Venezuela are as rich as those in other parts of the New World, but the country fell behind during the Neo-Indian epoch and its aborigines never attained the stage of civilization that was reached in Mexico and Peru. They did not develop cities, monumental architecture, or the writing, metallurgy, and fine weaving that characterize the more civilized Indians to the west. Nevertheless, as this volume will illustrate, they did produce a number of respectable forms of art, especially in ceramics, and their ceremonial objects are also worthy of study.

Venezuela has attracted some attention because of its geographical position midway between "Nuclear America," i.e., the areas in which civilization developed in the west, and the less advanced areas of eastern Latin America, which had only tribal cultures (Willey, 1960b, Fig. 2). Venezuela forms the connecting link between these two major parts of the New World, and knowledge of its archaeology is therefore essential for an understanding of developments within each of them.

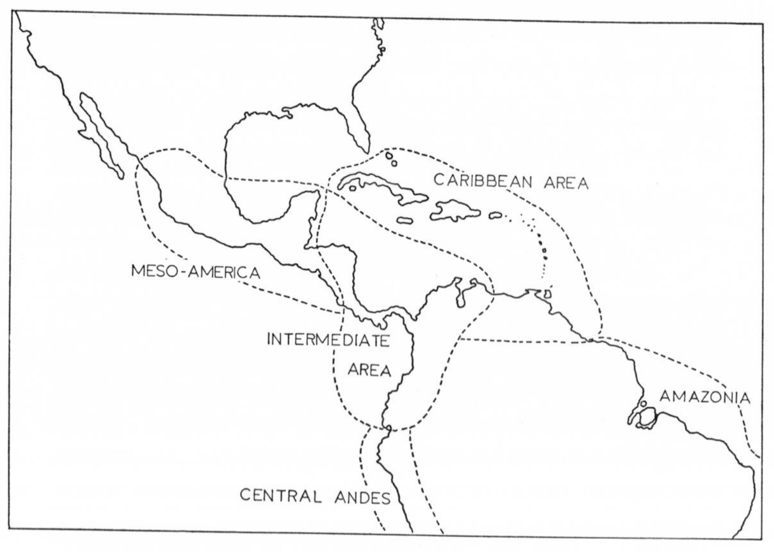

Fig. 1. Areas of cultural development in tropical America

Archaeologists now divide Nuclear America into three great areas of cultural development (Fig. 1):

1. Meso-America. Includes the southern two-thirds of

Mexico and the northern half of Central America, which were the seats of Mexican Indian civilization.

2. The Central Andes. Comprises the coastal and Andean parts of Peru, together with highland Ecuador and the northwestern part of Bolivia, where the second great series of Indian civilizations developed during prehistoric time.

3. The Intermediate area. This is the region between (1) and (2), centering in Colombia and also including southern Central America, coastal Ecuador, and western Venezuela. For some reason, its inhabitants failed to achieve civilization, despite contacts with their civilized neighbors to the north and south.

In eastern Latin America, we may distinguish two major areas of cultural development which impinge upon Venezuela (Fig. 1):

1. The Caribbean area. Includes the West Indies, the eastern half of Venezuela, and the northern half of the Guianas.

2. Amazonia. Comprises the basin of the Amazon River in Brazil and the neighboring countries, among them southern Venezuela.

A major difference between Nuclear America and the eastern part of Latin America is that maize was the principal crop cultivated in the west (along with potatoes in the higher parts of the Andes), whereas manioc was the staple food in the east. This distinction holds true for Venezuela. The western part of the country, which belonged to the Intermediate area, emphasized maize, whereas the eastern and southern parts of the country, which belonged to the Caribbean area and to Amazonia respectively, emphasized manioc.

It is now believed that effective agriculture utilizing maize had its origin in Meso-America and that it spread southward into western South America at the beginning of the Neo-Indian epoch. By the time of Christ, it had become the basic means of subsistence in Meso-America, the Central Andes, and the Intermediate area, including western Venezuela (Braidwood and others, 1962, pp. 171–72).

According to Sauer (1952, p. 46), manioc was domesticated in Venezuela, but this is less certain than the origin of maize. By the beginning of the Neo-Indian epoch manioc had apparently become the staple food of eastern Venezuela and by the time of Christ it was spreading to the rest of the Caribbean area and to Amazonia (Braidwood and others, 1962, p. 56).

Other elements of culture show a similar dichotomy. As this volume will illustrate, the pottery of western Venezuela is related to the ceramics of the rest of the Intermediate area, especially to that of Colombia and Central America, whereas the pottery of eastern Venezuela is related to that of the rest of the Caribbean area, including the West Indies and British Guiana. Similarly, western Venezuela shares a number of types of figurines, amulets, and other ceremonial objects with the Intermediate area, but such objects are virtually absent from eastern Venezuela and the rest of the Caribbean area.

Osgood (in Osgood and Howard, 1943, p. 5) has likened this situation to the shape of the letter *H*. The left upright of the *H* symbolizes Nuclear America, with its development based upon maize agriculture. The right upright signifies eastern Latin America, where the staple food was manioc. Venezuela forms the crossbar connecting these two lines of development, and hence its archaeology offers the best opportunity to determine the relationships between them.

But Venezuela cannot be considered merely a passive link between the two lines of development. At the points where the crossbar of the letter *H* joins the uprights, in both western and eastern Venezuela, the country has had an opportunity to contribute positively to the two lines of development. We have seen that the domestication of manioc may have been one such contribution; we shall attempt to demonstrate others during the course of this volume.

C. VENEZUELA AND ITS REMAINS

The country of Venezuela has a varied topography (Vila, 1960, pp. 13–15). Five major regions may be distinguished:

the Islands, the Coast, the Mountains, the Llanos, and the Orinoco River (Fig. 2). Ideally, we should also include the Venezuelan parts of Guiana and Amazonia, known as Guayana and Territorio Amazonas respectively, but they are too poorly known archaeologically.

Within the five topographic regions, sites tend to occur in clusters. In part this is due to the fact that archaeological research has been done more intensively in some areas than in others, but it apparently also reflects a tendency on the part of the Indians to concentrate upon the areas most favorable for habitation. Since the modern Venezuelans have also tended to concentrate in these places, there is a certain correspondence between the present population centers and those of the Indians. This being the case, it is convenient to apply the names of the modern population centers to the local concentrations of archaeological sites. Several areas of concentration are known from each major region (Fig. 2):

1. The Islands. A number of island groups off the Caribbean shore, between the Dutch islands of Aruba, Curaçao, and Bonaire on the west and the British Commonwealth islands of Trinidad and Tobago on the east, belong to Venezuela. Archaeological materials are available from two of these groups: Los Roques, which is off the central part of the coast; and Margarita, Cubagua, and Coche, which form a cluster off the east coast. We shall refer to the latter as the Porlamar area, after its present population center.

2. The Coast. Since the major part of our joint work has been concentrated on the coast, we have been able to distinguish the largest number of areas there—a total of ten. They are named after modern cities and towns, extending from Maracaibo, in the basin of the same name on the Colombian frontier, to Güiria, on the Peninsula of Paria opposite Trinidad. A third important area is Puerto Cabello, in the center, which has the easiest access to the mountains.

3. The Mountains. These comprise not only the Venezuelan section of the Andes, stretching northeastward from the Colombian border to the central coast, but also the Cordillera del Caribe, paralleling the central coast. The Cordillera Oriental, along the east coast, is too poorly known to be discussed here. Three areas may be distinguished in the high, southern part of the Andes; two in the lower Andes and foothills to the north and east; and three in the Cordillera del Caribe. The most important is

Fig. 2. Topographic regions and archaeological areas in Venezuela

the Valencia area, comprising the basin of the same name at the point where the Andes join the Cordillera del Caribe, behind the coastal area of Puerto Cabello.

4. The Llanos. East and south of the mountains is a large expanse of low land, extending up to the Orinoco River, which is known as the Llanos. Relatively little work has been done here, and we are able to distinguish only three areas: Barinas in the west and San Fernando and Valle de la Pascua in the center. Efforts to find significant archaeological sites in the eastern Llanos have so far proved to be unsuccessful.

5. *The Orinoco.* It has been customary to divide the land along the Orinoco River into three parts: upper, middle, and lower Orinoco (e.g., Howard, 1947, p. 40). Here, we shall instead distinguish four concentrations of sites, naming them after modern settlements: San Fernando and Puerto Ayacucho in the upper part of the valley, Parmana in the middle, and Barrancas in the lower part. The last has been the most intensively studied because of its apparent relationships with the West Indies and British Guiana.

Turning to the kinds of remains which occur in these regions, we may note first the presence of several kill sites, where the Paleo-Indians butchered their game (Pl. 1). The remainder of the Paleo-Indian sites consist of small deposits of worked and unworked stones, lying on the surface of the ground unaccompanied by any food debris. These may either have been camp sites or workshops (Pl. 2).

The great majority of the Meso- and Neo-Indian sites are places of habitation. Some are so small and shallow that they, too, may have served as camps, but most are large and deep enough to indicate the presence of more or less permanent villages (Pl. 5, A). All contain fragments of implements and utensils, and most have food remains as well, primarily shells and fish bones on the islands and along the coast, and animal remains in the interior. Hearths and burials are found in the refuse both on the coast and in the interior. These burials rarely contain grave objects.

The only other type of site which may possibly be common to both Meso- and Neo-Indians is the petroglyph, or rock carving (Pl. 10, A). Designs are sometimes also painted on cave walls or in rock shelters (Pl. 10, B).

The remaining kinds of sites appear to be limited to the Neo-Indian and Indo-Hispanic epochs. Both in the Valencia basin of the central mountains and on the western and central Llanos, there are mounds of earth, known on the Llanos as *medanos* (Pl. 11, C). These did not all accumulate as refuse heaps, like the shell middens; some were intentionally erected by the Indians to raise their houses and burials above the floods which prevailed on the Llanos during rainy seasons. Traces of a pile dwelling were found in one mound; apparently the Indians subsequently covered the piles with dirt to raise the ground to the level of their houses (Bennett, 1937, pp. 81–83).

Long causeways of earth, called *calzadas,* are known from the Barinas area in the western part of the Llanos (Pl. 11, A, B). These were presumably constructed to serve as roads while the surrounding plains were flooded during the rainy season (Cruxent, 1952). Aboriginal ditches and rock basins, of unknown significance, have been reported from various parts of the country (Pl. 10, E). Mortars and grooves for honing celts were also cut into living rock (Pl. 10, F).

Many of the leveled fields in the Andes, around which are piled stones cleared from the soil, were originally constructed by the Indians; these have been termed *poyos* (Febres Cordero, 1920, p. 15). The Andean Indians also dug *mintoyes,* or stone-lined shafts, each with a chamber extending to one side at the base (Pl. 10, D). They used these either as granaries, for storing potatoes, or as tombs, depositing pottery vessels, figurines, and pendants in them, along with the corpses (op. cit., p. 10). The term *mintoy,* as well as *santuario,* is also applied to caves in the Andes which the Indians used for ceremonies or for burials. These have yielded a rich harvest of pottery vessels, idols made of stone or clay in the form of figurines, and various ornaments, especially bat-wing pendants of stone or shell (Pl. 29, B).

The Spaniards introduced true masonry construction. This has been well studied at the site of Nueva Cadiz, on Cubagua Island, which was the first town established by Europeans in South America (Pl. 48). Several crude stone walls, notably at Vigirima in the Valencia basin (Pl. 10, C), are believed to have been erected by the Indians, but their use is not known.

Since our excavations have been conducted primarily in refuse of habitation rather than in the more elaborate structures just described, for reasons that will be given below, it seems advisable to say a few words about the artifact content of refuse deposits in Venezuela. The sites of the different epochs vary greatly in this respect. The Paleo-Indian sites have yielded unusually large numbers of stone artifacts, including projectile points, knives, scrapers, and choppers (Pl. 3). Marked bones have also turned up at one site (Pl. 4), but there are no clay or shell artifacts, or any objects of art.

By contrast, artifacts are rare in the Meso-Indian middens, and it is necessary to dig a great deal to obtain an adequate sample of artifacts. There is, however, greater variety than in the Paleo-Indian sites, including not only crude chips which could have been used as knives and scrapers but also bone points, shell gouges and pendants, biconical objects of ground stone, etc. (Pls. 7, 8). Stone projectile points are almost nonexistent in the coastal middens, but have been found at an interior Meso-Indian site in the eastern part of the country (Pl. 6). Clay pottery is known only from two interior sites in the west (Pl. 9).

The Neo-Indian refuse is exceedingly rich in pottery, of great variety and some complexity, but other types of artifacts are even more difficult to find than in the Meso-Indian sites. There are many different kinds, e.g., stone and shell celts, stone beads and pendants, and bone points, but these are so rare that Neo-Indian archaeology has to be done primarily in terms of its pottery (Pls. 12–47).

Chapter 2

APPROACHES TO VENEZUELAN ARCHAEOLOGY

A. DEVELOPMENT OF THE ARCHAEOLOGY

Here we will mention only a few of the people who have practiced archaeology in Venezuela; the reader is referred to our technical monograph for a more detailed account (Cruxent and Rouse, 1958–59, 1961). Adolfo Ernst and Vicente Marcano stand out as pioneers in the field. Ernst became the first director of the Museo de Ciencias in the 1880's and, like his contemporaries in other countries, occupied himself with all facets of natural history, including archaeology. He published descriptive studies of the collections that were beginning to accumulate, especially from the Andes (e.g., Ernst, 1886).

Vicente Marcano was the first to dig systematically in Venezuela. In 1887 he excavated several mounds at the eastern end of Lake Valencia in the Cordillera del Caribe. The report of his work was written by his brother, Gaspar Marcano (1889).

Tulio Febres Cordero (1920) and Mario Briceño Irragory (1928) followed Ernst in studying the collections. Both had an interest in history and attempted to identify the artifacts made by the tribes mentioned in the sources.

Luis R. Oramas (1917) and Alfredo Jahn (1931) were the principal excavators during the first decades of the twentieth century. Starting with the mounds of the Valencia basin, they extended their work east and west through the mountains, and Oramas also dug on the western Llanos. Like Marcano before them, their principal aim was to collect artifacts and to identify the Indians who made them.

In 1930, Dr. Rafael Requena became interested in the mounds of Lake Valencia and put Professor Mario del Castillo to work digging there. He subsequently described the material that was found in *Vestigios de la Atlántida* (1932), which, despite some rather wild speculations, attracted much interest and greatly stimulated the development of Venezuelan archaeology. His son, Antonio Requena (1947), continued his activity in the field.

Rafael Requena also invited three prominent North American archaeologists to excavate in Venezuela. At his request, Wendell C. Bennett, of the American Museum of Natural History, dug one of the Valencia mounds in 1932; Cornelius Osgood, of Yale University, excavated another in 1933; and Alfred Kidder II, of Harvard University, worked in both the Valencia basin and the Andes during successive field trips in 1933 and 1934 (Bennett, 1937; Osgood, 1943; Kidder, 1944). These archaeologists introduced the technique of artificial stratigraphy, which had been developed in the United States during the previous decade; they dug not simply to obtain specimens but to distinguish cultural differences and to date the sites in terms of these differences.

Osgood returned to Venezuela in 1941 with George D. Howard, an Argentine studying at Yale. They undertook a systematic survey of the archaeology of the country, making test excavations in four of the five topographic regions: Coast, Mountains, Llanos, and the Orinoco Valley. Their publication provided the first comprehensive, overall view of the archaeology of the country (Osgood and Howard, 1943). Howard subsequently followed up this work by digging intensively at Ronquín on the middle Orinoco River (Howard, 1943).

In 1945, Walter Dupouy, Antonio Requena, and Cruxent

made a similar series of intensive excavations in the newly discovered site of El Palito on the central coast. This was the first use of the stratigraphic method by local Venezuelan archaeologists and the results have proved to be very important for the establishment of a chronology in Venezuela.

The collaboration which has resulted in the present volume began during the summer of 1946, when Rouse stopped off in Caracas on his way to Trinidad and Cruxent and he collected briefly at several sites in the vicinity of the city. Rouse returned in 1950 and the two of us dug extensively, using the stratigraphic method at Manicuare on the east coast, at Barrancas on the lower Orinoco River, and near Barquisimeto in the Andes. The idea of a general monograph on Venezuelan archaeology, designed to bring Osgood and Howard's previous survey up to date and to establish an overall chronology for the country, took shape during a subsequent visit by Cruxent to the United States and was carried out during three additional trips by Rouse to Venezuela in 1955, 1956, and 1957. During these trips, we did additional field work in order to fill gaps in our knowledge, check doubtful points, and in particular to obtain charcoal for radiocarbon dating by the Geochronometric Laboratory at Yale University. Rouse returned to Venezuela again in 1961 and 1962 to collaborate on the present volume and to do additional field work.

Finally, it is important to note a visit to Venezuela by Clifford Evans and Betty J. Meggers, of the U. S. National Museum. Invited by Cruxent to follow up discoveries he had made in the San Fernando area on the upper Orinoco River and its tributary, the Ventuari, they dug there with him during the winter of 1957 (Evans, Meggers, and Cruxent, 1959). This work provides our first detailed knowledge of the archaeology of southern Venezuela and thereby complements the joint research of the present authors in the rest of the country.

B. TRIBES VS. CULTURES

As in other parts of the world, the approach to Venezuelan archaeology has changed radically during the past few years.

Until the 1930's, as we have seen, archaeology was done by collecting specimens indiscriminately and by subsequently identifying the tribes who made them through reference to the historic sources. The modern trend is to excavate stratigraphically in order to determine the "cultures," i.e., the ethnic groups, that occupied a particular site.

The method of tribal identification has proved to be unsatisfactory for several reasons. The sources are frequently so imprecise that they permit contradictory identifications; e.g., a recent conference on Lesser Antillean archaeology ended in complete disagreement as to which remains were produced by the Island Arawak tribe and which by the Island Carib (Société d'Histoire de la Martinique, 1963). Moreover, the method works well only for the Indo-Hispanic epoch, to which the sources refer. As one moves back in time through the Neo-, Meso-, and Paleo-Indian epochs, the method becomes more and more difficult to use, since the tribes and linguistic groups become more and more different from the ones which existed during historic time. Indeed, it is practically impossible to identify the tribes and languages which existed during the Paleo- and Meso-Indian epochs and therefore, with the discovery of remains of these epochs in Venezuela, the method of tribal identification has become impracticable.

In its stead, the archaeologists of Europe and America are now accustomed to establish purely archaeological units of culture, distinct from the tribes mentioned in the historic sources (e.g., De Laet, 1957, pp. 83–92; Willey and Phillips, 1958, pp. 21–24). In this approach, it is advisable to concentrate upon the remains of prehistoric communities, and in particular upon the refuse of habitation left by each community, which yields knowledge of a greater range of the community's activities than, e.g., a petroglyph or a cave shrine. The problem is to extract from the refuse criteria that may be used to group the communities into units which will serve as substitutes for the tribes of ethnology.

To do this, one must excavate the refuse stratigraphically, i.e., by dividing the excavations into arbitrary sections and levels. Then the material from each section and level may be compared to determine whether the site has been occupied by a single community or by several successive communities, each with its own distinctive culture. One may find, for example, that the lower level of a site represents a different community from that of the upper level, or that the sections at one end of the site were occupied by a later community than the sections at the other end of the site, and that each of these communities had a distinct culture.

Comparing communities at different sites which have been identified in this manner, archaeologists find that many of them share the same culture, i.e., that they had the same kinds of implements and utensils, the same means of subsistence, the same settlement pattern, the same religious objects, etc. We may say that such communities constitute a single "culture" and may name it after a typical site, either the one in which it was first encountered or the one in which it is best represented (Childe, 1956, p. 16).

Archaeologists frequently use various technical terms for the units which have just been discussed. In the United States, for example, it has become customary to refer to archaeologically defined communities as "components." The culture which is shared by a group of communities is known variously as a "complex," "focus," "phase," "style," or "industry" (Rouse, 1955, pp. 713–14).

To a considerable extent, the latter variation in terminology reflects differences in the criteria which archaeologists have used to group the components together into cultures. For example, Paleo-Indian archaeologists prefer the term "complex" because it indicates that they have defined their cultures in terms of a combination of types of implements which recurs from one site to another. French Paleolithic archaeologists prefer the term "industry" because they rely mainly on methods of manufacture.

In our technical monograph and in this volume, we use the term "complex" for the Paleo- and Meso-Indian units, for the reason stated above; but we employ "style" for the Neo-Indian and Indo-Hispanic cultures in order to indicate that those units are defined primarily in terms of ceramic traits. It would have been practically impossible for us to apply other criteria since, as already noted, there is little but pottery in the Neo-Indian and Indo-Hispanic sites.

In effect, each Paleo- and Meso-Indian complex consists of a particular combination of types of implements that recurs from one component to another, i.e., in several different communities, and that therefore permits us to classify the components, and through them the communities, as a single unit. Each style similarly consists of a recurrent combination of ceramic traits, whether of material, shape, or decoration, which forms the basis for a similar grouping of Neo-Indian or Indo-Hispanic components, and hence of communities.

Recently Watson Smith (1962) proposed the term "school" in place of "style." This has the advantage of focusing attention upon the people who made the pottery, i.e., on the community which, as we have seen, is basic to the concept of style. Nevertheless, we continue to use "style," since it might confuse readers if we used terms different from those in our technical monograph.

It should be recognized that the concept of complex or style replaces that of tribe in the previous approach to Venezuelan archaeology and that these two concepts are analogous: just as a tribe consists of a series of historic communities which have similar customs, a common language, and usually a single government, so a complex or style refers to a series of prehistoric communities (components) that shared many customs (types of artifacts, settlement patterns, etc.), though not necessarily the same language or government.

C. CHRONOLOGY

It is easy to determine when tribes existed by reading the dates given for them in the sources, but one cannot date complexes or styles in the same way, unless one is fortunate enough to be able to identify an Indo-Hispanic site mentioned in the sources. Otherwise, one must use purely archaeological methods to establish a chronology.

The best way to do this is to find a component representing one complex or style underlying a component of another such culture, in which case one may conclude that the culture of the lower component was earlier than that of the upper component. It is also possible to relate the remains of various complexes or styles to geological events known to have taken place at different times. For example, Kidder was able to correlate the La Cabrera style with a period in which Lake Valencia was rising, whereas the Valencia style lies on terraces formed when the waters subsequently fell; and hence we can say that the La Cabrera style is earlier than the Valencia style (Chaps. 5; 7, A, C).

In the absence of stratigraphy or of the possibility of relating archaeological finds to geological or historical events, the archaeologist must fall back upon a technique known as "seriation." In its most general sense, this simply means placing a number of components (and, through them, their complexes or styles) in a logical order. For example, one may find the remains of style A at one end of a site and of style B at the other end, with little or no admixture, in which case one may say that the people of styles A and B occupied the site at different times. However, one will not know whether style A or B came first, unless and until one is able to relate them to another phenomenon that has been dated. If, for example, one finds European trade objects in association with style A but not with B, then one can say that style B preceded A at the site.

The technique of seriation works best within individual sites, as in the example just given, because there is little possibility that different components could have coexisted at the same site. If one applies the technique more widely to a number of neighboring sites, as we do in the present volume, one must watch out for the possibility of coexistence and, whenever it occurs, abandon seriation, since the technique is based upon the assumption that the units seriated have followed each other in time. The larger the area covered, the greater is the possibility of coexistence, and therefore the technique cannot be used beyond the limits of a restricted locality.

A special form of seriation has been developed in the United States, primarily by James A. Ford (1949), in which pottery is first classified into units known as types. This is done primarily in terms of material, in order to be able to utilize plain potsherds as well as those bearing traces of shape and decoration. The archaeologist then determines the relative popularity of the various types in each of his components by calculating their percentages, and arranges the components in order of increasing or decreasing popularity of the types, charting the percentages on a graph, component by component (e.g., Evans and Meggers, 1960, Fig. 48). This method has proved to be very useful for making fine divisions of time within individual styles or within a series of related styles. Since, however, we are here concerned with the definition of styles and with their broad-scale relationships, we have not used the method in our studies. Its application will come later, in the next stage of Venezuelan archaeology, when attention is turned from broad-scale correlations to working out the details of the sequences in each locality.

By use of the methods just described, the archaeologist is able to build up a sequence of complexes and styles within each locality, extending from the beginning of its occupation by man to the present time. He must then "synchronize" the sequences in different areas by comparing their complexes and styles to determine which ones are contemporaneous. If a pair of these cultures occur in the same relative position in two local sequences, if they share traits which are likely to have spread from one culture to another, and especially if one contains objects which seem to have been traded from the other, then the archaeologist may conclude that they are contemporaneous. Sometimes he is able to check his synchronizations by correlating them with historic or geological events; e.g., two of our Meso-Indian complexes, Cubagua on the island of the same name and El Heneal on the central coast, are associated with a period when the sea was at least 50 cm. lower than it is today, and hence we may say that they are approximately contemporaneous.

The best way to express the relative ages of complexes and styles is to plot them on a chronological chart. One makes a vertical column for each of the local sequences and moves the complexes and styles up and down in the columns until they are at the proper levels to indicate contemporaneity and differences in age. Our technical monograph contained five such charts, for the Venezuelan islands, coast, mountains, Llanos, and the Orinoco respectively (Cruxent and Rouse, 1958–59, Figs. 7, 26, 100, 149,

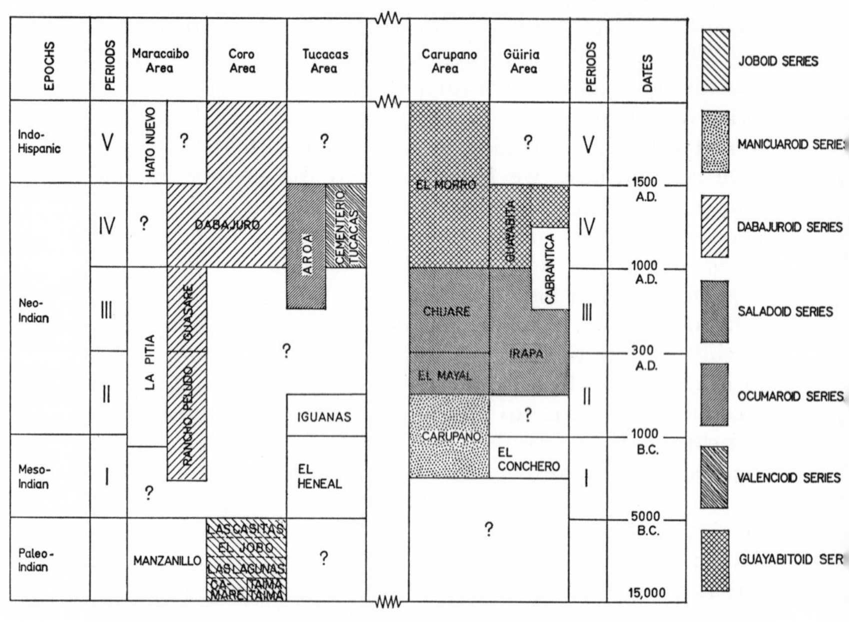

Fig. 3. Relative chronology of the eastern and western coasts of Venezuela

and 170). Figure 3 illustrates the method and presents a revised version of the eastern and western ends of the coastal chart, where our research since the monograph was published has produced significant changes.

On both sides of Figure 3 is a succession of five roman numerals which refer to a series of arbitrary periods set up to express the relative ages of the various complexes and styles; they enable us to say, for example, that two styles were both in existence during Period II or that a given style persisted from Period II into Period III. In effect, this is the archaeologist's way of saying that a certain tribe lived during the eighteenth and nineteenth centuries; it provides him with a relative time scale to use in place of the Christian calendar.

The four great epochs in the Indian occupation of the New World which were outlined at the beginning of this book may now be dated in terms of our relative time scale. As shown in Figure 3, the Paleo-Indian epoch lacks a corresponding period because it had not yet been discovered when we set up the time scale. The Meso-Indian epoch corresponds to Period I; the Neo-Indian epoch, to Periods II–IV; and the Indo-Hispanic epoch, to Period V.

Until recently, we have had no adequate way of converting the relative time scale into the Christian calendar, although we have tried several means of estimation, which need not be detailed here. Now, the method of radiocarbon dating gives better results. During the course of atomic research, chemists discovered that all living matter contains a form of carbon known as carbon 14. So long as organisms are alive, they will have the same relative amount of carbon 14; and when they die, it decomposes at a constant rate, which has been calculated experimentally and confirmed by measurements of historically dated objects, e.g., Egyptian mummies. To determine how much time has passed since an organism died, therefore, it is only necessary to extract its carbon, measure the percentage of carbon 14 in it, subtract this from the percentage in living organisms, and divide the result by the percentage of carbon 14 which decomposes each year (Libby, 1955).

Thanks mainly to the Geochronometric Laboratory at Yale University, which has analyzed most of our radiocarbon samples, we now have a series of 57 dates for Venezuela, which are listed in the Appendix. These dates make it possible to assign absolute values to the relative periods, as shown in Table 1.

The time of the Paleo-Indian epoch is considered questionable because it is based upon only three analyses, one of which is poorly associated with the epoch. The subsequent dates become increasingly reliable as one moves toward the Indo-Hispanic epoch.

TABLE 1. ABSOLUTE DATES OF EPOCHS

Epoch	*Period*	*Absolute Date*
Paleo-Indian	—	15,000–5000 B.C.(?)
Meso-Indian	I	5000–1000 B.C.
Neo-Indian	II	1000 B.C.–300 A.D.
" "	III	300–1000 A.D.
" "	IV	1000–1500 A.D.
Indo-Hispanic	V	1500 A.D. to present

As the Appendix illustrates, the dates are given to us with a margin of error, preceded by the symbol ±. This reflects the fact that the dates have been obtained by counting the radioactivity of the samples and are therefore subject to the inaccuracies inherent in any counting procedure. Indeed, there are only two chances in three that each date actually falls within the margin of error given in the Appendix, but there are five chances out of six that it falls within double that margin. Hence, some archaeologists prefer to double the margin of error given by the laboratories.

The dates contained in the Appendix are also subject to weaknesses in the nature of the sample itself. Any organic material may be used, but charcoal is the least likely to have been contaminated by chemicals in the soil and therefore we have limited ourselves to this material. There are in addition problems of relating the charcoal samples to the proper cultural material, which will be discussed in the text where they are pertinent (e.g., Chap. 4, D).

In view of all these possibilities for error, it is unlikely that radiocarbon dates will ever replace relative periods in prehistoric archaeology. We shall have to continue to use the two together, relying more on the relative periods than on the dates.

D. SERIES

In forming our chronological charts, we encountered many cases in which one complex or style seemed to have developed into a second, the second into a third, etc. Archaeologists are accustomed to refer to such sequences of cultures as "traditions" (Willey, 1945). We also noted instances in which a complex or style in one area appears to have given rise to a similar culture in another area; the second culture in turn to a new one in a third area, etc. Archaeologists term such occurrences "horizons" (op. cit.). In our technical monograph and in this volume, we use the term "series" to cover both kinds of occurrences, since in our opinion they are aspects of the same phenomenon: in both cases, a number of complexes or styles have come to resemble each other, either because many of their characteristics have persisted through time or because those characteristics have spread from one place to another through space.

Seven of the series are shown on the chronological chart (Fig. 3) by means of different kinds of shading. We have named each series by selecting a typical complex or phase and adding the suffix "oid" to its name. For example, the Joboid series is composed of the Camare, Las Lagunas, El Jobo, and Las Casitas complexes, which succeeded each other in the Coro area. (This happens to be the only series which is entirely included in Fig. 3; the rest all extend into areas not covered there.) Figure 3 also illustrates the fact that not all complexes and styles can be assigned to series. Eventually, it may be possible to do so, but Venezuelan archaeology has not yet reached that stage in its development.

It is easy enough to conceive how a series could have arisen within a single area, as, e.g., in the case of the Joboid sequence. The original complex or style would gradually have changed as time passed until it became a new one, retaining only a portion of its original traits, and the same process would have been repeated again and again. The process was probably hastened in many cases by the adoption of new traits from other areas which replaced those previously existent in the local area.

The spread of a series from one area to another is a more complicated process. It may have resulted from a migration, i.e., the local people may have moved en masse from the first area to the second, in which case the complexes or styles in the two regions will be very similar, if not identical. On the other hand, traits of the first culture may have spread to the second with little, if any, accompanying movement of people, in which case the two cultures will not be so much alike.

Sometimes, the diffusion of traits from one area to another—and often into a third and fourth area as well—will have been strong enough to cause a sharp break between the receiving culture and its predecessor. In other cases, the influences will have been weaker, with the result that the receiving culture will show a mixture of traits from the originating culture with traits which have survived from its own predecessor in the local area. In such cases, we may say that there has been a fusion of the series previously present in the local area with the series which has diffused into that area.

Styles resulting from the fusion of series are often difficult to classify. There are three possibilities: (1) If traits of the local series continue to predominate, we may assign the style to that series. (2) If traits of the intrusive series are in the majority, the style has to be assigned to that series. (3) If new traits, resulting from the fusion, predominate, then a new series has arisen. The Chuare and Irapa styles of Figure 3 illustrate alternative (1); they are Saladoid but show strong influences from the Barrancoid series. Examples of the other two alternatives will be given later (Chap. 7, A, B, and C, D).

Once a series has become established in several different areas, it may persist in those areas for a considerable period of time, especially if its possessors maintain contact and are able to exchange ideas and customs. Even when contact has been broken, they may continue to develop similar customs, since their common cultural background will tend to channel the changes in the same direction. Eventually, however, they will diverge and, in so doing, may form new series. (For an example of this process, see Chap. 8, A and Fig. 31.)

When archaeologists discover cultural similarities between two or more areas, such as are presented by our series, some prefer to explain these similarities by invoking the theory of parallel development that has just been discussed. Other archaeologists explain the similarities by postulating a migration from one area to another (cf. Comas, 1959). We have attempted to avoid these two extremes by interpreting each of our series without prejudice in favor of either theory and by considering all other possible explanations for the similarities, such as diffusion of individual traits from one culture to another without movement of people.

We have also taken into consideration the fact that similarities can arise without any contact whatsoever between cultures, either because two groups of people have reached the same stage of cultural development, have adapted in the same way to similar environments, or because they happen to have otherwise made the same choice from among a limited set of possible solutions to a cultural problem that has arisen within their respective cultures. This is another reason why it is difficult to trace the prehistory of tribes or language groups in terms of archaeological remains; similarities in the remains do not necessarily indicate the spread of a tribe or group from one area to another or its persistence from one period to another.

In the case of several of our series, we have decided not to make a choice between the various possible explanations of cultural similarity because we do not possess enough data to be able to do so prudently. We have, in particular, preferred not to postulate long-range migrations when we cannot base them on a more or less continuous series of complexes or styles, covering the extent of the presumed migration.

We have discussed the series in some detail because they

will be the basic unit in the following presentation of the results of our study of Venezuelan archaeology. In a summary volume such as this, we cannot go into the details of the individual complexes and styles. We can only discuss and illustrate the major series and the most important independent complexes and styles.

Chapter 3

PALEO-INDIAN EPOCH

The beginning of the Paleo-Indian epoch, which precedes Period I in our relative chronology, has been fixed by three radiocarbon dates, of 14,920, 12,780, and 12,380 B.C. respectively (Appendix, M-1068, O-999, Y-1108-IV), at about 15,000 B.C. The epoch lasted until the start of the Meso-Indian epoch ca. 5000 B.C.

The Paleo-Indians lived under very different climatic conditions than those which prevail today. The temperature was somewhat lower, but not so much so as in North America, where the last great ice sheet still covered much of the continent (Flint, 1957, Pl. 3). As a result, the present areas of snow on the peaks of the Sierra Nevada de Mérida in the Venezuelan Andes extended to lower altitudes than today, and there were glaciers on the higher mountain peaks, including several in the vicinity of Caracas (Royo y Gómez, 1956, pp. 201–02). The temperature at sea level was probably still quite warm, however.

The sea stood at a lower level at this time, for an appreciable part of its water was locked up on the land in the form of the great ice sheets of the Northern Hemisphere. The Gulf of Paria, which now separates the island of Trinidad from eastern Venezuela, was largely dry, Trinidad formed part of the mainland, and the Orinoco River discharged its waters only through the southern part of its present delta (Andel and Postma, 1954).

During the ice ages, tropical areas such as Venezuela were sometimes subject to greater rainfall than at present, i.e., they were in a pluvial stage of climate (Zeuner, 1959, pp. 265–74). Forests were then more widespread than at present and even the areas which are now arid must have consisted of woodlands interspersed with savannas. The existence of these conditions has been demonstrated by studies of fossil bones and pollen from the Paleo-Indian site of Muaco in the Coro area of western Venezuela (Royo y Gómez, 1960b).

Roaming the forests and savannas, until desiccation caused them to become extinct (op. cit.), were many large mammals, such as the mastodon, megatherium (a giant sloth), and the horse. These animals are supposed to have supplied the Paleo-Indian with his major source of food. He probably also ate wild plant foods; there is no evidence that he did any fishing.

A. JOBOID SERIES

The only Paleo-Indian series so far defined is that which Cruxent discovered in 1956 at El Jobo in the interior of the state of Falcón, i.e., in the Coro area (Fig. 2). The area is at present arid but, as we have seen, it seems to have been more humid during the Paleo-Indian epoch. One can imagine that at that time there were large expanses of forests separated by grasslands. Large mammals such as the mastodon must have abounded in such a climate, and man must have come there in some numbers to hunt the mammals.

The quantity of remains discovered by Cruxent indicates this. Within the valley of the Río Pedregal, in an area of some 1000 sq. km., he has located more than 45 sites and has collected 20,000 artifacts. These were eroding out of the surface and lay concentrated in small areas, each of which may have been the site of a camp or a workshop (Pl. 2). There were no traces of burial or any animal remains, except for two unidentifiable pieces of bone.

At only one place did Cruxent find any remains beneath the surface. This was at Sanjón Malo, in the bottom of the valley, where artifacts from upstream had been redeposited by the river. Excavating here, Cruxent found artifacts to a depth of 1.75 m.

Wolf Petzall, geologist of the Creole Petroleum Corporation and the Universidad Central de Caracas, has collaborated in the study of the El Jobo sites. He believes that the terraces of the Río Pedregal offer the best opportunity to determine the relative age of the complex, since there are five or six of these terraces and they all bear artifacts. As for the absolute age of the complex, after examining Cruxent's excavation in the material redeposited by the river at Sanjón Malo, which dates from the middle period of terrace formation, Petzall concluded that the process of redeposition must have required thousands of years "and possibly more than 10,000 years" (Petzall, MS, p. 9).

Cruxent collected two charcoal samples from El Jobo sites, which were analyzed in the Geochronometric Laboratory at Yale University. Unfortunately, both were modern in age; apparently they had been deposited by the present inhabitants of the area (Appendix, Y-438, Y-439).

From a detailed, continuing study of the artifacts, in an attempt to develop a precise classification and to correlate the artifacts with the terrace system of the Río Pedregal, as suggested by Petzall, Cruxent finds reason to group the sites into four successive complexes: Camare, Las Lagunas, El Jobo, and Las Casitas, which are limited to the highest (and hence the earliest), the upper middle, lower middle, and lowest terraces respectively. Together, these four complexes comprise the Joboid series (Fig. 4).

Crude chopping tools, made by battering a piece of quartzite with another stone in order to knock off flakes and thereby to sharpen the edges of the original stone, are characteristic of the entire Joboid series (Fig. 5, A). Larger flakes struck off the pebbles were also used after further trimming, the thinner ones probably as knives (Fig. 5, B) and the thicker ones probably as scrapers (Fig. 5, D). Typically, the scrapers have a plano-convex shape; their lower surface is smooth and flat while the convex upper surface bears irregular scars that have resulted from rechipping. No artifacts of bone or shell have been recovered.

The Camare and Las Lagunas complexes, of the upper terraces, lack projectile points of stone. Presumably the Indians of these complexes made their spears entirely of hard, tropical woods, shaping the points with their scrapers and perhaps hardening them in the fire. The Camare sites

EPOCHS	PERIODS	CORO AREA	PERIODS	DATES
Indo-Hispanic	V		V	1500 A.D.
Neo-Indian	IV		IV	1000 A.D.
	III		III	300 A.D.
	II		II	1000 B.C.
Meso-Indian	I		I	5000 B.C.
Paleo-Indian		LAS CASITAS EL JOBO LAS LAGUNAS CAMARE		15,000

Fig. 4. Chronology of the Joboid series

have yielded only large chopping tools, scrapers, and knives (Pl. 3, B). The Las Lagunas artifacts are smaller and include a new type—bifacially worked blades, which may have been used as hand axes or knives or else have been hafted in thrusting spears (Pl. 3, C, D).

Stone projectile points begin with the El Jobo complex. They are made almost entirely of quartzite, are lanceolate

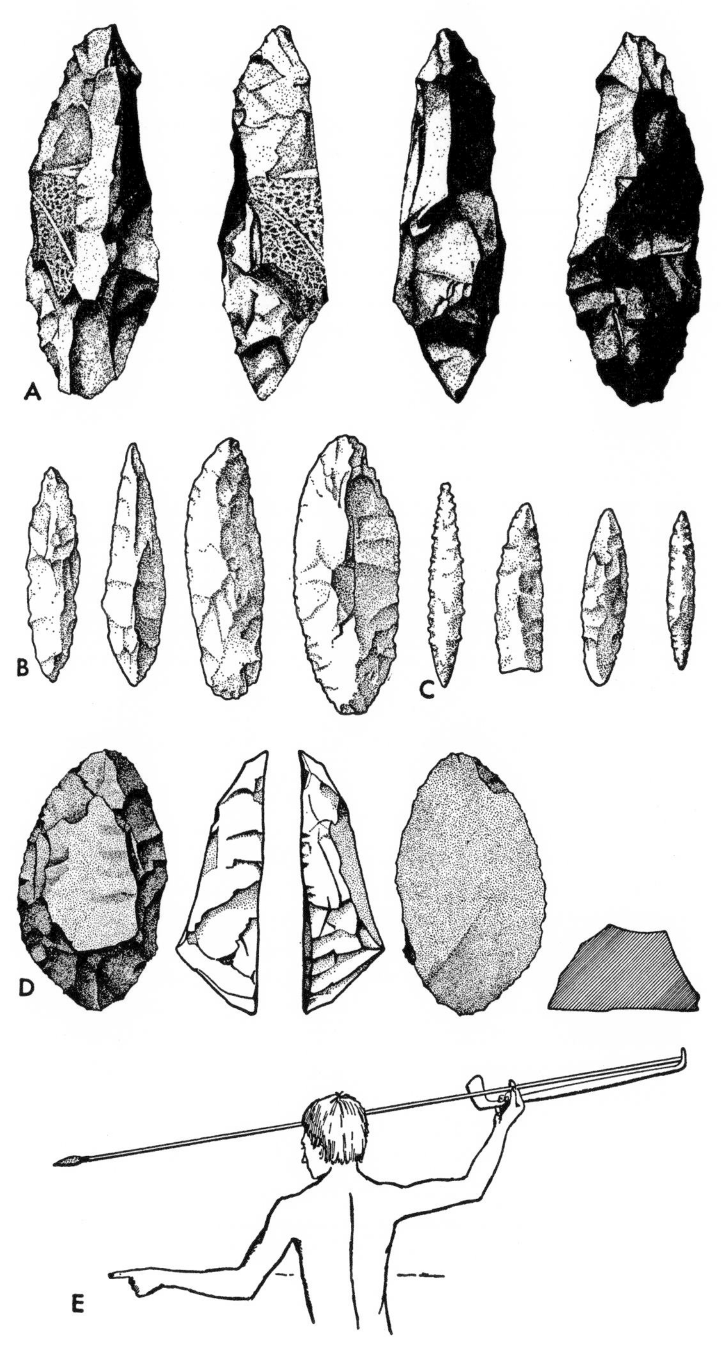

Fig. 5. Artifacts of the El Jobo complex and use of spear thrower

in shape, lenticular in cross section, and usually have a rounded base (Fig. 5, C). Their surfaces are rather coarsely chipped but the edges have been finely trimmed and are sometimes serrated (Pl. 3, E, F). Occasionally the bases are flat or concave rather than rounded.

Evidence from Gypsum Cave in the western part of the United States, where artifacts were preserved under conditions of extreme aridity, indicates that the Paleo-Indian projectile points were hafted in wooden, feathered shafts in order to form darts or throwing spears (Harrington, 1933, Fig. 51). In North America, at least, these were used with a spear thrower, which consisted of a handle that could be hooked into the butt end of a spear as shown in Figure 5, E. In effect, this lengthened the hunter's arm and thereby improved the accuracy and force of his throw.

The El Jobo type of point continues into the Las Casitas complex, of the lowermost terraces, but to it is added another type of point, having a triangular blade and a stem at its base, by means of which it was attached to the shaft (Pl. 3, G). This new type of point is in the minority.

The Joboid sequence is in accord with the latest discoveries in both North America and the southern part of South America, where it is also beginning to appear likely that a stage without stone projectile points preceded that with points of stone (Sellards, 1960; personal communications from Alex D. Krieger, Eduardo Mario Cigliano, Dick Edgar Ibarra Grasso, and Edward T. Lanning). Some archaeologists (e.g., Willey, 1960a, pp. 116–17) have suggested that the gathering of wild vegetable foods was the principal means of subsistence in this stage before the appearance of stone points, but we think it more likely that the earlier Joboid Indians had projectile points of a perishable material, such as wood, and that they relied as much upon hunting as the later Indians who possessed stone points. As already indicated, the scrapers of the earlier Joboid complexes can best be interpreted as tools for working wood, e.g., in making spears; they are too large and coarse for use in scraping skins.

The lanceolate points of the El Jobo complex are quite

similar to specimens found with a mammoth at Santa Isabel de Ixtapan in the Valley of Mexico (Avelyra A. de Anda, 1955, Pl. 25: 1, 2). Comparable material also occurs in the United States; e.g., Alex D. Krieger (personal communication) informs us that the Weiser River site in western Idaho "has almost every trait that El Jobo has, even the specific scraper and projectile-point forms." In the other direction, he notes that "the specific El Jobo point type and the specific forms of scraper found at El Jobo also occur all the way to southern Argentina and Chile." The point type, for example, is common in the Ayampitín I complex of central Argentina, which has a radiocarbon date of 7970 ± 100 years ago (González, 1952, pp. 110–17; Schobinger, 1959, p. 39, Fig. 2, top). We must await further discoveries in the intervening areas before commenting on the significance of these resemblances.

The stemmed points of the Las Casitas complex, finally, may be compared to those of the Ayampitín II complex of central Argentina (Schobinger, 1959, Fig. 2, bottom). Schobinger (op. cit., p. 37) has suggested that stemmed points may have survived in Argentina until the advent of pottery. We would not be surprised if this had also happened in Venezuela, for we found a stemmed point in our excavations at Punta Gorda, on Cubagua Island in the Porlamar area, dating from the second half of Period II and coinciding with the first appearance of pottery on the island (Chap. 4, B). In addition, Cruxent has discovered a workshop in which stemmed points were made near the rapids of Atures in Territorio Amazonas, southern Venezuela, accompanied by a number of potsherds of unidentified style.

Following Schobinger's theory, we tentatively conclude that only lanceolate points—the El Jobo type—are characteristic of the Paleo-Indian epoch in Venezuela and that triangular, stemmed points represent a survival of the Paleo-Indian form of life into the Meso-Indian epoch. From this point of view, the few stemmed points which Cruxent found in the Las Casitas complex on the lowermost terraces of the Río Pedregal, accompanied by a much larger number of lanceolate points, would represent the end of the Paleo-Indian epoch and the beginning of a transition to the Meso-Indian epoch, in which stemmed points gradually came to predominate (Fig. 4).

B. OTHER FINDS

Since the preparation of our technical monograph, four additional Paleo-Indian deposits have been discovered, at Muaco, Taima Taima, Manzanillo, and Rancho Peludo. We can discuss these only in a very preliminary manner, since they are still under study. There is also a fifth site, Canaima, but consideration of this will be deferred until the Meso-Indian chapter, since it has yielded only stemmed points and therefore, according to our hypothesis, represents a survival of the Paleo-Indian way of life into the following epoch.

Muaco. From 1952 until his death in 1961, José Royo y Gómez (1960a, b), geologist of the Universidad Central in Caracas, studied a deposit of vertebrate fossils at Muaco, near La Vela de Coro, not too far east of the mouth of the Río Pedregal, on the upper part of which the Joboid finds were made. The site lies around a spring, ascending funnel-like through a deposit of mud 2–3 m. deep. Throughout the mud are bones of extinct animals, which apparently came to the spring to drink and died there (Pl. 1, B). Reptiles, birds, and mammals are all represented, among them such extinct forms as the mastodon, megatherium, and a New World horse. The animals are adapted to a humid climate; and the accompanying flora could likewise have flourished only under moist conditions, according to pollen studies by E. Medina and S. Steinhold. Such conditions have not been present since the time of the final Pleistocene glaciation; and therefore Royo y Gómez (1960b, p. 32; 1960c, p. 154) attributes the deposit to the late Pleistocene.

The upper part of the deposit, to a depth of 0.5 m., has been heavily eroded and weathered (Royo y Gómez, 1960a, p. 502). Here and in the spring itself, one finds the bones of modern animals and remnants of European artifacts, such as glass bottles, for the spring still serves as a source of drinking water for the inhabitants in the vicinity. But the greater part of the deposit appears to have remained undisturbed since late glacial time.

Learning of the site from a previous report of Royo y Gómez (1956, pp. 206–07), Cruxent decided to excavate in the hope of finding traces of early man. In 1959, he dug a trench 20 x 12 m. to a depth of 2.5 m. in an undisturbed part of the site and was successful in finding artifacts, as well as other evidences of Paleo-Indian activity (Cruxent, 1961). Some bones of the extinct animals had been broken in order to extract the marrow or, in the case of crania, the brain. Many bones had been burned. Others are grooved, as though they had been cut by man (Pl. 4, A), and still others show traces of use as anvils (Pl. 4, B, C).

A fragment of a lanceolate point of the El Jobo type was obtained in situ, among the bones of extinct mammals, and another complete point was found eroding out of the deposit. Also in situ were a piece of a plano-convex scraper, like those found in all the Joboid complexes, a possible knife, and a number of hammerstones.

This is a typical kill site, where the Paleo-Indians came to hunt because the animals could more easily be approached while they were drinking than at other times. Presumably the projectile points were used to dispatch the animals, which were then cut up with the knife; the skin and bones were cleaned with the scraper, and the bones were broken with the hammerstones. The large bones that bear traces of cutting may have served as chopping blocks, upon which the meat was cut up. As is usual at kill sites, there are no traces of habitation; the Indians apparently cut up the meat in order to carry it more easily to their camps, which were situated elsewhere.

Thanks to the Creole Petroleum Corporation, fragments of burned bone were analyzed in the laboratory of its affiliate, the Humble Oil Company. They yielded a date of 14,920 B.C. (Appendix, O-999). Subsequently, other bone from the same site was dated, by the University of Michigan laboratory, at 12,780 B.C., as stated at the beginning of this chapter (Appendix, M-1068).

At first glance, it might seem that the dates refer to the El Jobo complex, since all the diagnostic traits of that complex were found at Muaco. However, there is an alternative possibility, that Indians of the Camare and El Jobo complexes successively visited the site and that the dates refer to the former complex rather than to the latter. It is impossible to decide between these two alternatives because objects tend to move up and down in deposits of mud, like that at Muaco, and one cannot be certain whether the radiocarbon samples were associated with the two fragments of projectile points or not.

Taima Taima. During March 1962, Cruxent discovered another site similar to Muaco at Taima Taima, 1750 m. east of the former. Excavation of this site has only begun (Pl. 1, A) but already there have been found bones of extinct animals broken by man, several pitted stones, and a series of stones which may have been used as club heads. The edges of these show traces of battering through use, but little, if any, evidence of manufacture. Cruxent also obtained a crude scraper, unlike those at El Jobo. He encountered a concentration of material which looked like charcoal but which proved upon analysis to be coal (Appendix, Y-1199).

Manzanillo. Cruxent had learned previously of the existence of deposits of fossil wood on the Peninsula of Guajira, north of the city of Maracaibo (Fig. 2). He attempted to follow up this report, on the assumption that the Paleo-Indian would have favored the use of fossil wood for his artifacts, but was unsuccessful until a former student of his, Eddie Romero, happened to notice fossil wood in Manzanillo, a suburb of Maracaibo. Here Cruxent (1962) found implements of fossil wood and unworked stones eroding out of the surface of the ground over a limited area. There were no bones or shells. Projectile points were also lacking; the artifacts consisted of a few chopping tools and a larger number of scrapers, all made of fossil wood. The formlessness of the artifacts is noteworthy; they show little regularity of shape (Pl. 3, A). Presumably they are related in a general way to the Camare complex (Fig. 3).

Rancho Peludo. At Rancho Peludo, to the northwest of Maracaibo, the writers found four implements of the Manzanillo type eroding out of the bank beneath a ceramic deposit, which will be discussed in later chapters (4, D; 6, A). Here it need only be noted that a charcoal sample from the base of the ceramic deposit yielded a date of 12,380 B.C. (Appendix, Y-1108-IV). Since this is within the range of the Paleo-Indian epoch, we doubt that it applies to the ceramic deposit. Instead, this sample may originally have been associated with the Manzanillo-type implements and have been brought up to the level at which we found it by the later, ceramic Indians while digging graves (Rouse and Cruxent, 1963). Further excavation is planned at Rancho Peludo to test this possibility.

Chapter 4

MESO-INDIAN EPOCH

The Meso-Indian epoch corresponds to Period I of our relative chronology. We possess eight radiocarbon dates for it in Venezuela, of which the oldest are 3800, 3770, and 3400 B.C. for the Cerro Iguanas site in the Tucacas area of the west coast and 2325 B.C. for the Punta Gorda site on Cubagua Island in the Porlamar area (Appendix, Y-853, Y-854, Y-497). These dates are supported by one of 5060 B.C. for Cerro Mangote, a Meso-Indian site in Panama (Cruxent and Rouse, 1958–59, Table 3). As a result, we place the start of the Meso-Indian epoch about 5000 B.C., though it may actually have begun earlier. It ended about 1000 B.C. with the first appearance of intensive agriculture in Venezuela.

By 5000 B.C., the glacial and pluvial conditions of the Paleo-Indian epoch had given way to a climate very similar to that of today. The temperature may have been slightly warmer than at present, in which case the snow line would have been somewhat higher on the slopes of the Sierra Nevada de Mérida than it now is (Jahn, 1931). The rainfall probably approximated that of the present time.

Melting of the glaciers in the Northern Hemisphere caused a rise in the level of the sea. It was still below its present level during the first part of the epoch, however, for the refuse in our earliest sites, Cerro Iguanas and El Heneal in the Tucacas area and Punta Gorda and La Aduana on Cubagua Island, extends to a maximum depth of 50 cm. beneath the present level of the sea. There is evidence that, as the water subsequently rose, Cerro Iguanas became an island in a coastal lagoon, separated from the sea by an offshore sandbar. Still later, during the Neo-Indian epoch, the lagoon silted in and became a mangrove swamp (Rouse, Cruxent, and Wagner, MS).

It should be noted that the rise of sea level was not the only factor affecting the shoreline. The coast of Venezuela from the Río Chico area westward was gradually rising at this time, and the coast to the east was falling (Royo y Gómez, 1956, p. 199). Cubagua and Margarita Islands were likewise rising. These changes must have partially nullified the effect of the rise in sea level at Cerro Iguanas, El Heneal, Punta Gorda, and La Aduana.

Further east, the Gulf of Paria grew almost to its present size as a result of the rise in sea level and, possibly, a fall in the land. Trinidad became separate from the mainland, but the Orinoco River continued to discharge only through its southern mouths, not into the gulf, so that the gulf's waters were still considerably more saline than at present (Andel and Postma, 1954, p. 142).

The mastodon and other large Pleistocene mammals had become extinct, forcing the Meso-Indian to look for other sources of food. He undoubtedly continued to hunt the smaller surviving animals, but these did not supply enough meat to serve as the main source of food except in limited areas of the interior, if we may judge by the disappearance of projectile points in most parts of the country. Only in Venezuelan Guayana, at the side of Canaima mentioned in the previous chapter, do we find stone projectile points in large enough numbers to indicate survival of the Paleo-Indian form of life.

On the coast, the Meso-Indians shifted from the Paleo-Indian form of life to one based upon sea food, and as a result they left large middens, or refuse heaps, consisting primarily of marine shells, fish bones, and the remains of echinoderms. Stone projectile points are virtually absent, and in their place one finds points of bone, which were probably used as parts of arrows or of hooks for catching fish. The large shell heaps are easy to find, and as a result we have been able to learn a great deal about the Meso-Indians of the coast. We can distinguish one series of complexes, the Manicuaroid, and know of a number of other complexes which cannot yet be assigned to series.

The emphasis upon fishing along the coast had an important consequence. It caused the Meso-Indians living there to acquire a familiarity with the sea and, apparently, the ability to navigate, which enabled them for the first time to colonize the islands offshore. The earliest remains not only on the Venezuelan islands but also in the West Indies date from this epoch, and there is some indication, which we shall discuss in the following pages, that the Indians who produced these remains came primarily from the coast of Venezuela.

Back from the coast, except in the areas of Paleo-Indian survival, it is probable that the Meso-Indians came to rely more upon wild vegetable foods than upon either game or seafoods, if we may judge by the situation in other parts of America which have a similar environment, e.g., the Tehuacan valley, Mexico (MacNeish, 1962). Unfortunately, traces of this kind of life are difficult to find because of the absence of sea shells. We know of only two possible sites: Michelena in the Valencia basin, where pestles and a milling stone occurred with traces of habitation; and Capacho in the San Cristobal area of the Andes, where non-ceramic refuse lies beneath a ceramic deposit (Fuchs, 1960).

From the collecting of wild plants to their domestication is only a short step. MacNeish's (1962) excavations in the Tehuacan valley have shown that maize and other plants had been domesticated there by the middle of our Meso-Indian epoch. Evidence has also accumulated, e.g., at Huaca Prieta and related sites, that agriculture had reached Peru by 2500 B.C. (Braidwood and others, 1962, p. 168).

It must be stressed that the sites mentioned had only a

rudimentary form of agriculture. The yield of crops was probably not very great, in terms of the effort required, and so we may assume that wild plants continued to be the main source of food, supplemented by hunting and fishing. Archaeologists call this primitive form of agriculture "incipient," in order to distinguish it from the intensive agriculture which prevailed during the Neo-Indian epoch (e.g., Willey, 1960b, Fig. 2).

Theoretically, the Venezuelan Indians who lived back from the shore and subsisted primarily by the gathering of wild vegetable foods should have acquired incipient agriculture before the close of the Meso-Indian epoch. There are two possible sources: (1) Maize and associated crops may have spread to western Venezuela from further west in South America where, as we have seen, these crops became widespread at a relatively early date. (2) The Meso-Indians of eastern Venezuela may themselves have domesticated manioc, as suggested by Sauer (1952, p. 146).

Pottery occurs in most of the sites of incipient agriculturalists that have been found in the western part of Latin America—the later Tehuacan finds, the Monagrillo complex of Panama, Barlovento and Puerto Hormiga in Colombia, and the Valdivia complex of Ecuador—whereas it is absent from the purely hunting, fishing, and gathering complexes (Willey, 1960a, p. 125). These sites have radiocarbon dates ranging from 3000 to 2000 B.C. (op. cit.; Rouse and Cruxent, 1963). If, therefore, we are to search for the remains of Meso-Indian agriculturalists in Venezuela, we ought to look for pottery-bearing sites that date from the second millennium B.C. and lack evidence that cultivation was the principal means of subsistence.

At the time we wrote our technical monograph, we knew of no such remains. Since then, Cruxent discovered and we have excavated the ceramic site of Rancho Peludo in the interior of the Maracaibo area, which meets the requirements; and Gallagher (1962) believes he has found a comparable deposit at the base of the shell heap of La Pitía, not too far away (Fig. 3). As a result, we now possess for the first time evidence of all four of the patterns of life supposed to have been present in Venezuela during the Meso-Indian epoch, of the Paleo-Indian survivors, coastal fishermen, gatherers back from the shore, and incipient agriculturalists. We shall consider each of them in turn.

A. PALEO-INDIAN SURVIVALS

The site of Canaima is situated on a savanna west of the Salto de Hacha, some 4 km. from Canaima in the state of Bolivar (Fig. 2). Since it lies in the middle of Venezuelan Guayana, it is really beyond the scope of the present paper, but we include it anyway because it is our only good example of survival of the Paleo-Indian way of life into the Meso-Indian epoch.

The site was studied by Cruxent in October 1959. It is a workshop or camp site, like those at El Jobo, and its artifacts lie on the surface mixed with pieces of laterite. The artifacts are made almost exclusively of jasper, which abounds in the region. They include triangular projectile points with stems and barbs, scrapers, and hammerstones. The projectile points resemble those found as a minority on the lowermost terrace at El Jobo and the scrapers are plano-convex, as at El Jobo (Pl. 6). There were no artifacts of bone, shell, or pottery.

It is presumed that the stemmed points were hafted in throwing spears, like those used during the Paleo-Indian epoch, for these points are considerably larger than modern arrow points. They are even more numerous than the projectile points at El Jobo, and from this fact we deduce that the Canaima Indians subsisted primarily by hunting the smaller game which inhabited the savanna.

The age of the complex is unknown. We have already given our reasons for assigning it to the Meso-Indian epoch: because stemmed points did not begin to appear until the very end of the Joboid Paleo-Indian sequence; because a single stemmed point was found at the Meso-Indian site of Punta Gorda; and in particular because stemmed points have been found in association with Meso- or Neo-Indian pottery at the rapids of Atures in Territorio Amazonas.

The Canaima complex was probably widespread throughout the Guianas, for isolated finds of stemmed points have been made at various places in both Venezuelan and British Guiana (Dupouy, 1956, 1960; Evans and Meggers, 1960, pp. 21–24). We do not know how long it lasted, but eventually the spear gave way to the bow and arrow and the blow gun and, with this, the Paleo-Indian way of life, as we define

EPOCHS	PERIODS	ISLANDS: Porlamar Area	COAST: Cumaná Area	COAST: Carúpano Area	PERIODS	DATES
Indo Hispanic	V				V	
						1500 A.D.
Neo-Indian	IV				IV	
						1000 A.D.
Neo-Indian	III				III	
						300 A.D.
Neo-Indian	II	PUNTA GORDA		CARUPANO	II	
						1000 B.C.
Meso-Indian	I	MANICUARE / CUBAGUA	MANICUARE	CARUPANO	I	
						5000 B.C.
Paleo-Indian						
						15,000

Fig. 6. Chronology of the Manicuaroid series

it, came to a close. Hunting did not cease, however, for there are still tribes along the upper Orinoco and its tributaries who subsist mainly by hunting. Unfortunately, we do not yet know anything about the immediate antecedents of these tribes; our archaeological knowledge of the hunting peoples stops with the Canaima complex.

B. MANICUAROID SERIES

Turning to the new modes of life which developed during the Meso-Indian epoch, we shall consider first the coastal fishermen. Here, we have been able to distinguish a single series, consisting of four complexes: Cubagua, Manicuare, Punta Gorda, and Carúpano. It is known only from the eastern coast and the adjacent islands (Fig. 6). Since it centers on the islands and on the Peninsula of Araya, which is likewise offshore, there must have been a strong maritime emphasis.

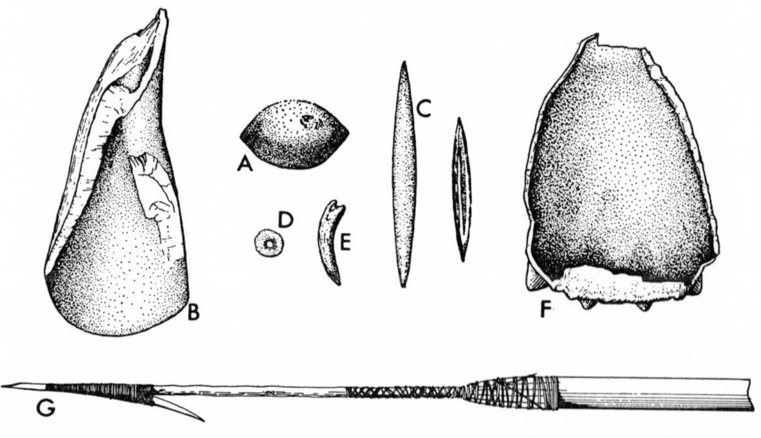

Fig. 7. Artifacts of the Manicuare complex and possible hafting of bone point

The sites of the Manicuaroid series consist of large piles of shells and other remnants of seafood. A human burial was found in one of these shell deposits; it lacked grave objects. The most distinctive artifacts of the series are projectile points of bone, which are believed to have been hafted in arrows or harpoons, like those still made along the upper Orinoco River (Fig. 7, G). They were presumably used in fishing and possibly also for hunting. There are also small bipointed stones which could have been employed in hunting, either in slings or as parts of bolas; alternatively they might have had some sort of ceremonial function (Fig. 7, A). Finally, the series is characterized by flat milling stones, which may well have been used with grinders to prepare the maguey plant, since this is still a major source of food at the present time.

The series is named after the site of Manicuare on the Peninsula of Araya, opposite the city of Cumaná, where we first excavated it in 1950. It is best known, however, from the great shell heap at Punta Gorda on Cubagua Island, where one of our trenches, dug in 1956–57, reached a depth of 4 m. (Pl. 5, A). We encountered the Cubagua complex at the bottom of this midden, the Manicuare complex in the middle part, and the Punta Gorda complex at the top. The Cubagua complex yielded a radiocarbon date of 2325 B.C., and the Manicuare complex, dates of 1730 and 1190 B.C. (Appendix, Y-497, Y-295, Y-296g). The Punta Gorda complex is not dated directly but contains trade pottery of the El Mayal style, which has an age of A.D. 100 (Appendix, Y-297). This places it in our Period II, and hence in the Neo-Indian rather than the Meso-Indian epoch, but it may more conveniently be discussed here since it represents a survival of the Meso-Indian way of life into the Neo-Indian epoch.

The main difference between these three complexes is an increasing use of shell for the manufacture of artifacts. The Cubagua complex has only cups (Fig. 7, F), hammers, and a disk of shell. To these are added in the Manicuare complex shell gouges, consisting of segments from the outer whorl of the conch shell beveled to form a bit but otherwise unground (Fig. 7, B; Pl. 7, A), shell beads (Fig. 7, D), and shell pendants, which typically are shaped like an incisor tooth (Fig. 7, E; Pl. 7, C). In the Punta Gorda complex there are also shell projectile points, made like the bone points, shell celts, and a more elaborate form of pendant. A single stone point was found here; as already noted (Chap. 3, B), this can be considered intrusive, possibly from the Canaima complex.

The addition of the shell gouge seems to us particularly

significant. The original, Cubagua complex contains no artifacts that could have been used for making dugout canoes, from which we deduce that the Indians must have traveled from the mainland to the islands by means of rafts. The addition of the gouge in the Manicuare complex must have made possible the manufacture of dugout canoes, which would have been a great advantage for a maritime people.

Little is known about the fourth complex of the Manicuaroid series, Carúpano. It was found underlying two successive ceramic styles in our 1955 and 1957 excavations at the El Mayal 1 site in the Carúpano area, farther east along the coast (Fig. 3). We include it in the Manicuaroid series primarily because of the presence of shell gouges.

The Manicuaroid series is believed to have been a local development. It well illustrates the Meso-Indian movement from the coast of Venezuela onto the adjacent islands (Fig. 6). Whether this movement continued out into the West Indies is a moot question. No Meso-Indian sites have yet been found in the Lesser Antilles. They do occur in the Virgin Islands, Puerto Rico, the Dominican Republic, and Haiti, but with very different artifacts than those of the Manicuaroid series. Not until one reaches Cuba, the island farthest from Venezuela (Fig. 1), does one again find shell gouges and other artifacts like those at Manicuare. It is possible that similar finds will eventually be found in the intervening region. As an alternative possibility, Rouse (1960, pp. 23–24) has suggested that Manicuaroid Indians may have accidentally been blown directly to Cuba by storms, by-passing the remaining islands. Other archaeologists (e.g., Alegría, 1955) prefer instead to derive the Meso-Indians of Cuba from Florida, where somewhat similar artifacts are also to be found.

C. OTHER NON-CERAMIC FINDS

Coastal complexes. Two additional coastal complexes are believed to date from Period I—Cabo Blanco in the La Guaira area and El Heneal in the Tucacas area, both a considerable distance west along the coast from the Manicuaroid series (Fig. 2). Cabo Blanco is too poorly known to be worth discussing here. By contrast, Cruxent has extensively excavated two sites of the El Heneal complex, the type site and a large shell heap at Cerro Iguanas, a short distance farther west. At El Heneal, the results were disappointing in terms of artifacts; he obtained only a few hammerstones, a pitted stone, and several edge grinders, so-called because the grinding facets are on the edges rather than on the sides of the artifacts, as is usually the case. There was a greater yield at Cerro Iguanas, including crude stone celts and a long bone pin (Pl. 8, A, B). One charcoal sample from El Heneal and three from Cerro Iguanas have been analyzed in the Yale laboratory, yielding dates of 1550, 3770, 3400, and 3800 B.C. respectively (Appendix, Y-455, Y-852 to Y-854).

Edge grinders similar to those of the El Heneal complex have been found in the shell heap of Cerro Mangote in Panama and, underlying pottery, in Loiza cave, Puerto Rico. At Cerro Mangote, they have a radiocarbon date of 5060 B.C. (Cruxent and Rouse, 1958–59, Table 3). The significance of these resemblances is unknown.

Interior finds. The Michelena complex consists of part of a milling stone, two pestles, two grooved stone axes, and a hammerstone which were found in ash-stained soil during excavation for a factory in the outskirts of the city of Valencia (Fig. 2). We possess no evidence as to the age of this material; we place it in Period I purely on the assumption that it preceded the appearance of pottery in Venezuela.

At Capacho, type site for the style of that name, in the San Cristobal area of the Andes (Chap. 6, A), Helmut Fuchs (1960), of the Museo de Ciencias Naturales in Caracas, recently found a non-ceramic deposit consisting primarily of snail shells beneath the ceramic layer. This deposit was subsequently excavated by Cruxent, Fuchs, and Erika Wagner, but the material has not yet been studied. We tentatively place it in Period I on the assumption that it may antedate the first appearance of pottery in western Venezuela.

D. BEGINNING OF THE DABAJUROID SERIES

Cruxent (1957) discovered a large village site at Rancho Peludo on the Río Guasare at the base of the Guajira Peninsula in the extreme western part of Venezuela (Fig. 3). We have already noted that there may be an earlier, Paleo-Indian deposit in this site, and are now concerned with the subsequent ceramic occupation. Urn burials, potsherds, and other refuse are eroding out of the river bank at a depth of 1.0 to 3.3 m. beneath the surface (Pl. 5, B). Digging there in 1957, Cruxent obtained charcoal which the Yale laboratory dated at 2820 B.C. (Appendix, Y-578). Since at the time this was the earliest date for pottery in the New World, it seemed desirable to check it, and so Cruxent, Rouse, and Maruja Rolando de Roche re-excavated the site in 1961, obtaining 12 additional radiocarbon samples, of which the Yale laboratory has dated 6 (Appendix, Y-1108 to Y-1110). The two earliest are believed to pertain to the Paleo-Indian deposit. The rest range from 1860 to 445 B.C. and apparently date Meso-Indians who had begun to make pottery (Rouse and Cruxent, 1963).

The pottery belongs to a series we call Dabajuroid, which was widespread through the Maracaibo basin and on the Caribbean coast during later, Neo-Indian time. Two styles of this series are represented at the site, but we are here concerned only with the first of them, which we have named Rancho Peludo (Fig. 8). Its sherds are moderately coarse-textured, thick, grit-tempered, and come from bowls with incurving rims or from ollas with necks that curve outward at the rim (Fig. 8, A; Pl. 9, E-G). Some of the vessels had rounded bases and others were provided with tall, flaring, annular bases, which were occasionally perforated (Pl. 9, A). The outer surfaces of the lower parts of the vessels had frequently been roughened by pressing fabrics or rubbing fingers into the wet clay (Fig. 8, B; Pl. 9, E). The necks sometimes bear one or two bands, produced by leaving a ridge where one of the coils of clay used in building up the wall of the vessel joins another. Otherwise, the only decoration consists of simple strips or lumps of clay applied to the surfaces, and gashes or punctations made by pressing a pointed tool into the clay. Most of the designs are geometric (Fig. 8, C; Pl. 9, C, D) but several have the form of human heads (Pls. 5, B; 9, B).

We found parts of two clay griddles, like those which the later, Neo-Indians of eastern Venezuela used to bake bread. These suggest that the inhabitants of Rancho Peludo had already begun to cultivate manioc, from the roots of

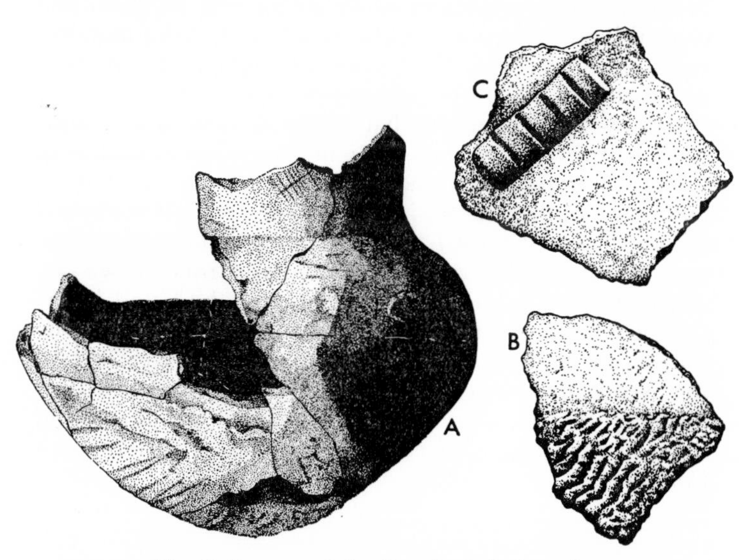

Fig. 8. Pottery of the Rancho Peludo style

which flour for bread was obtained, although they may instead have gathered wild manioc. In either case, we doubt that the plant was the major source of food, since griddles are so much less common than in the later, Neo-Indian sites. The Rancho Peludo Indians probably relied primarily upon game and wild vegetable foods, as Willey (1960a, p. 125) has postulated for the Monagrillo ceramicists of Panama and those of Valdivia in Ecuador.

E. OTHER CERAMIC FINDS

Another possible Meso-Indian ceramic deposit has just been identified. It lies at the bottom of the great shell heap of La Pitía near the base of the Peninsula of Guajira (see Chap. 6, D). In a preliminary report on his excavations at the site, Gallagher (1962) informs us that he was unable to find traces of agriculture in the bottommost refuse, but at the same time he compares his finds with those in the Meso-Indian ceramic sites of Colombia and Panama, and from this we may infer that a rudimentary form of horticulture was practiced. He has not yet described the pottery, and therefore we are unable to discuss it here.

It may be anticipated that other Meso-Indian ceramic styles will eventually come to light, in eastern as well as in western Venezuela, for the earliest Neo-Indian pottery in both parts of the country is so varied and so well made and decorated that it must have had a long history of development during the Meso-Indian epoch. In particular, we predict that Meso-Indian sites will eventually be found in the Orinoco basin with pottery from the beginning of the Barrancoid and Saladoid series, which are the earliest of the Neo-Indian series in that region. We shall see later (Chap. 7, A) that there is reason to regard the Barrancoid series as an offshoot of certain Meso-Indian pottery from Colombia.

Chapter 5

NEO-INDIAN EPOCH: INTRODUCTION

The beginning of the Neo-Indian epoch is placed at 1000 B.C. because that is the earliest date we have for intensive agriculture, associated with the Saladero style of pottery on the lower Orinoco River (Appendix, Y-42). The epoch ends with the arrival of Europeans around A.D. 1500.

Pottery provides a relatively sensitive indicator of chronology and, by studying it, we have been able to divide the Neo-Indian epoch into three parts, which comprise Periods II, III, and IV of our relative chronology. These three periods are purely arbitrary; the boundaries between them have been drawn where there happened to be breaks in our relative chronology and in the radiocarbon sequence, at A.D. 300 and 1000 respectively.

The climate was the same as it is today in Venezuela, except possibly for minor variations in rainfall, which are indicated by changes in the level of Lake Valencia. At present, the lake has an interior drainage—the water that flows into it evaporates so fast that the lake is unable to rise high enough to discharge through its natural outlet from the Valencia basin southward across the Llanos and thence into the Orinoco River (Cruxent and Rouse, 1958–59, vol. 1, pp. 163–69). But the archaeological site of

Los Tamarindos has yielded evidence that the level of the lake was rising during Periods II and III, presumably because increased rainfall brought in more water than was able to evaporate. Toward the close of Period III, the lake became so high that it overflowed its natural outlet and, for an undetermined period of time, discharged into the Orinoco basin. Then, probably at the beginning of Period IV, it began to fall again and resumed its interior drainage, gradually cutting a series of four terraces into its shores before it reached its present level (op. cit., Table 8). This fall is thought to have been due primarily to a decrease in rainfall; other possible factors are denudation of the hillsides by the Indians and tectonic movements which may have reduced the amount of land which drained into the lake.

The only other change in the environment which has come to our attention has to do with the level of the sea. According to Andel and Postma (1954, Table 7), the water in the Gulf of Paria had reached its present height by Period II. It fell slightly during Period III but returned to its present height in Period IV. Shortly after the beginning of Period IV, the Orinoco River broke through to form the Boca Vagre and began to discharge for the first time into the Gulf of Paria, killing the coral communities which could no longer exist there because the Orinoco's waters caused a marked decrease in the salinity of the gulf. Andel and Postma have concluded that there was a corresponding destruction of the shellfish communities in the gulf, but our excavations indicate that only certain species, such as the mussel, died out. We found shells of many other species in the Period IV middens, and the present inhabitants informed us that oysters, in particular, still grow along the Peninsula of Paria, especially during the winter dry season, when the saline content of the water rises because the Orinoco is no longer in flood (Rouse, Cruxent, and Wagner, MS).

It is not known whether the Paleo-Indian way of life survived into this epoch in the parts of Venezuela with which we are concerned. In any case it must have disappeared before the end of the epoch, for there is no mention of it during historic time. Possibly the Paleo-Indians moved further south in Guayana and Territorio Amazonas, where there are still a few hunting tribes, e.g., the Guaica.

The Meso-Indian way of life did survive throughout the epoch, and the early European explorers found Meso-Indians still living in certain out-of-the-way places, such as the Parajuano, who inhabited pile dwellings in the Lago de Maracaibo (Cruxent, MS), and the Warrau in the delta of the Orinoco River (Wilbert, 1956). We shall have something to say about the archaeology of these Meso-Indian survivors in the following pages.

The great majority of the inhabitants of Venezuela had reached the Neo-Indian stage of development by this time. Their agriculture had now improved to the extent that it became the principal means of subsistence, with hunting, fishing, and gathering relegated to a secondary position. There were larger, more permanent settlements; more elaborate pottery; and a series of ground stone artifacts, such as idols, which the Meso-Indians had been unable to make. The Neo-Indians constructed mounds, earth-, and stone-works and, especially in the western part of the country, produced a series of ceremonial objects, such as figurines and amulets of stone, bone, and shell, which are frequently found in graves and caves.

We are now able to recognize ten series of Neo-Indian styles and, through these series, are beginning to acquire some idea of the movements of people and interrelationships of culture during the epoch. The series provide partial answers to some important questions: In what parts of the country did the Neo-Indian way of life first arise? How and when did it spread to the rest of the country, replacing the previous Paleo- and Meso-Indian complexes? When did the cultural division between eastern and western Venezuela arise? What were the relationships between these two divisions and of each of them with the cultures of the neighboring countries? The remainder of the book will be devoted to these problems.

A. DIVISIONS OF NEO-INDIAN CULTURE

We have speculated that the cultivation of manioc may have been developing throughout Venezuela during the

Meso-Indian epoch, though we have evidence of it only at the site of Rancho Peludo. In that site, clay griddles indicative of manioc cultivation were replaced during the first part of the Neo-Indian epoch by metates and manos, which presumably served, as they still do in the area, to grind maize. This same change has been noted by Reichel-Dolmatoff (1957, pp. 233–34) at the site of Momíl in northern Colombia, which is roughly contemporaneous. Following his lead, we assume that, in western Venezuela as in Colombia, maize became the staple crop during the first part of the Neo-Indian epoch. It probably diffused from Meso-America, where it had first been domesticated, to Colombia and thence on into western Venezuela (see Chap. 1, B).

On the other hand, griddles of clay (*budares*) are characteristic of the Neo-Indian sites of eastern Venezuela and continue to be used today (though they are now made of iron) in the preparation of bread from the manioc root. Metates and manos—as distinguished from the more poorly formed milling stones and grinders of the Manicuaroid series (Chap. 4, B)—are lacking in the east. We conclude from these facts that, whereas maize became the staple food of western Venezuela, manioc survived in the east to become the staple food there.

This is, of course, a tenuous conclusion, since it is based upon indirect evidence. Nevertheless, as already noted (Chap. 1, B), there is other, more direct evidence of a dichotomy in Neo-Indian culture between western and eastern Venezuela. The two regions differ markedly in their pottery. Western Venezuela has vessels with legs and tall, perforated annular bases; a greater proportion of ollas and jars; plain rims or an occasional hollow rim; horizontal rod handles; incision without modeling; and red-and-black-on-white painting. Eastern pottery has plain or short, solid annular bases; a predominance of wide-mouthed bowls; rims elaborated with flanges, bevels, or ridges; vertical strap handles; modeled-incised lugs and figures on vessel walls; and white-on-red painting. The western painted designs are complex, including such motives as frets and ticked lines, whereas the eastern designs consist largely of simple lines. By contrast, incised designs are much simpler in the west than in the east.

Other aspects of culture support this dichotomy. Burial in the west was in shaft graves or urns, accompanied by many grave objects, whereas in the east the body was simply placed in the ground, usually without any grave objects at all. The western Indians built mounds and other earthworks; the eastern Indians did not. The western remains include a variety of ceremonial paraphernalia, such as clay figurines, incense burners, and pendants carved in the form of amulets, but these are almost entirely lacking in the east, where non-ceramic artifacts are more utilitarian, the principal types being clay pot rests (*topia*) and stamps. Caves were used as shrines in the west but not in the east.

These facts suggest that Neo-Indian culture developed separately in western and eastern Venezuela. We cannot yet pinpoint the origins of the two developments, nor do we know to what extent they have resulted from outside influences. All that can now be said is that the earliest Neo-Indian remains reveal the full dichotomy between the two.

But the line between the two developments is not a sharp one. There is a transitional zone in the middle of the country which has some traits of the west and some of the east. In the following discussion, therefore, we will distinguish a central as well as a western and an eastern division of Neo-Indian archaeology.

We should also note in passing that it would be possible to distinguish a fourth division, in the high Andes. The staple crop in that region was neither maize nor manioc but the potato. Certain other traits, such as the *poyos,* shaft graves, and cave shrines, recall the Andean sections of Colombia. Nevertheless, the pottery of the high Andes is related to, and appears to be derived from, the pottery of the rest of western Venezuela and so we prefer to include the high Andes in that division.

The three divisions will be considered separately in the following chapters. In each chapter we shall discuss only those series which appear to be indigenous to the division under consideration, ignoring the series which have intruded from another division. The chapter on western Venezuela will be concerned with three series, Dabajuroid, Tocuyanoid, and Tierroid; the chapter on central Venezuela, with five, Barrancoid, Arauquinoid, Valencioid, Ocumaroid, and Memoid; and the chapter on eastern Venezuela, with only two, Saladoid, and Guayabitoid. First, however, it is necessary to consider the Meso-Indian survivals with which these various series came into contact.

B. MESO-INDIAN SURVIVALS: WESTERN AND CENTRAL VENEZUELA

In all of western and central Venezuela, we have as yet found only a single site which extends from the Meso- into the Neo-Indian epoch. This is Rancho Peludo, near the Colombian border, where the Rancho Peludo style, presumably characterized by incipient cultivation of manioc, was replaced by the Guasare style, supposedly accompanied by intensive cultivation of maize, sometime after 445 B.C. to judge by our latest radiocarbon date for the Rancho Peludo style (Appendix, Y-1108-I). Both styles belong to the Dabajuroid series.

With this exception, we know nothing about the first millennium of the Neo-Indian epoch in either western or central Venezuela. We do not begin to have satisfactory evidence until the time of Christ. Whether the two divisions were inhabited only by Meso-Indians until that time or whether the Meso-Indians had been replaced at an earlier date by Neo-Indians, either wholly or in part, remains to be determined.

C. MESO-INDIAN SURVIVALS: EASTERN VENEZUELA

Eastern Venezuela has yielded much fuller information. Here, there is evidence from the very beginning of the Neo-Indian epoch, indicating that Indians of the Manicuaroid series and of other Meso-Indian complexes survived along the coast and on the islands, and that Neo-Indians of the Barrancoid and Saladoid series had already taken over the Llanos and the Orinoco valley respectively.

In discussing this evidence, it will be convenient first to consider the westernmost area, Barcelona, and then to examine the remaining four areas to the east, Porlamar, Cumaná, Carúpano, and Güiria (Fig. 2).

Barcelona area. In 1955 and 1957 we located and excavated a number of small shell heaps on islands in the coastal lagoon east of the city of Barcelona, which we group together as the Pedro García complex. We obtained a considerable variety of types of artifacts, including a bone point, an edge grinder, a conical pestle, several shell gouges, milling stones, and a series of stone chips. These indicate relationships with all the other non-ceramic complexes of Venezuela, but the nature of the relationships is not known, since the various types occurred in different sites and may not all belong to the same complex.

All of the excavated sites yielded pottery, but in such small numbers that we think it must have been obtained by trade instead of being manufactured locally. There is so little that it cannot be identified stylistically, but several of its traits are reminiscent of the Barrancoid series. Griddle sherds, which would have indicated agriculture, are absent, and we doubt that agriculture would have been feasible in this lagoon environment.

A charcoal sample from the type site of Pedro García was dated at 570 B.C. by the Yale laboratory (Appendix, Y-456). We have therefore placed the complex in the first part of Period II, but extend it through Period III, because the great variation within the complex suggests that it had a long duration (Cruxent and Rouse, 1958–59, Fig. 26).

The occurrence of Barrancoid traits in the presumed trade pottery is of interest because it supports the hypothesis, to be presented below (Chap. 7, A), that the Barrancoid people were already on the Llanos during the first part of Period II. From there, they could have easily traded northwards to the Meso-Indian survivors in the Barcelona area, which is not cut off from the Llanos by mountains; it is at the end of the only unbroken stretch of lowlands extending from the Llanos to the coast.

Porlamar—Cumaná—Carúpano—Güiria. Members of the

Manicuaroid series survived in all these areas except Güiria, as already noted (Chap. 4, B). If our chronology is correct, Manicuare, the second complex of the series, began in the Porlamar and Cumaná areas during the latter half of the Meso-Indian epoch, i.e., of Period I, and continued into the first half of Period II (Fig. 6). The Carúpano complex is presumed to have been contemporaneous with Manicuare. The final complex of the series, Punta Gorda on Cubagua Island, is dated in the latter half of Period II and therefore falls entirely within the Neo-Indian epoch.

Neither the Manicuare nor the Carúpano complex contains any evidence of contact with the Neo-Indians, though they partially overlapped the appearance of the latter in the Orinoco valley to the south. By contrast, some potsherds of Neo-Indian origin do occur in the Punta Gorda levels on Cubagua Island. These appear to be the result of trade with the El Mayal people of the Saladoid series, who had by now moved up from the Orinoco valley to the coast. It is interesting to note that this trade pottery consists largely of fragments of bottles, a fact which suggests that the Punta Gorda people readily accepted pottery for storing water, which was scarce on Cubagua Island, but did not use it for cooking.

It would seem, therefore, that the Manicuaroid people continued to live on the eastern coast and adjacent islands through the first half of Period II without coming into contact with Neo-Indians. In the latter part of Period II, they yielded possession of the coast to Neo-Indians of the Saladoid series but continued to live on the islands. Apparently, it was not until Period III that the Saladoid people continued on into the islands and replaced or fused with the Manicuaroid people there (Figs. 6, 28).

This conclusion is supported by the more limited evidence available from the Meso-Indian sites further east along the coast. At El Peñon, east of Cumaná, and at El Conchero, on the Peninsula of Paria in the Güiria area (Fig. 2), we discovered a pair of sites which yielded nothing in the way of artifacts except a large number of chips of stone, some of them quite small. Such chips are also characteristic of the Ortoire complex of Trinidad, which is radiocarbon dated at 880 and 890 B.C. (Rouse, 1960, pp. 10–12); and therefore we place El Peñon and El Conchero in the first half of Period II (Fig. 3). Neither at El Peñon, El Conchero, nor in the two sites of the Ortoire complex that have been excavated on Trinidad (Ortoire and St. John) are there any evidences of Neo-Indian contact. Hence, the Neo-Indians cannot have reached Trinidad either until the middle of Period II.

What is the reason for this delay in the Neo-Indian penetration of northeastern Venezuela—until the latter half of Period II on the coast and until Period III on the nearby islands? As will be explained in a later chapter (8, A), the Neo-Indians who came in with the Saladoid series were moving down the Orinoco River. They may have been delayed at its mouth, especially since the channels of the Orinoco delta now opening into the Gulf of Paria were closed at the time. After reaching Trinidad and the Peninsula of Paria, the Cordillera Oriental would have provided a further barrier. These mountains would be difficult for a riverine people to penetrate and on the north side of the Peninsula of Paria they come directly down into the sea, leaving no space for travel by land along the north short of the peninsula. To the west of the Cumaná area, the mountains similarly fall directly into the sea, impeding travel by land along the shore, and hence may have effectively cut off the Porlamar, Cumaná, and Carúpano areas from the rest of the country, permitting its Meso-Indian inhabitants to survive there in isolation while the Neo-Indians were expanding in the rest of the country.

Chapter 6

NEO-INDIAN EPOCH: WESTERN VENEZUELA

Western Venezuela consists of the Maracaibo basin, the section of the mountains to its south and east, and the coast to the north, extending from the Peninsula of Guajira on the west through the Coro area on the east (Fig. 2). The western part of the Llanos is also included. Three series, Dabajuroid, Tocuyanoid, and Tierroid, seem to have originated and to have centered here, though they are not limited to the region. As we shall see, all three of them expanded beyond it into central Venezuela and, in the case of the Dabajuroid series, to eastern Venezuela and the Dutch islands of Aruba, Curaçao, and Bonaire as well.

It is presumed that the development of Neo-Indian culture in this region was made possible by the spread of intensive cultivation of maize from Colombia and ultimately from Meso-America (see Chap. 5, A). In our technical manuscript we assumed that it entered the country with the Tocuyanoid series at the close of the first millennium B.C. The discovery of the Rancho Peludo site now offers an alternative possibility—diffusion to the Dabajuroid people during an earlier part of the first millennium. We do not yet possess enough information to be able to decide between these alternatives and shall have to consider them both.

The fact that we begin with the Dabajuroid series does not mean that we favor it, but simply that we have earlier dates for it.

A. DABAJUROID SERIES

As now known, the Dabajuroid series consists of two parts: (1) a local development (tradition) within the Maracaibo and Coro areas of the coast; and (2) a horizon which spread out from the final phase of the local tradition in two directions: (a) southward through the Lago de Maracaibo and up into the San Cristobal area of the Andes, and (b) eastward along the coast through the Puerto Cabello, Barcelona, and Cumaná areas and out to the islands in the Porlamar area (Fig. 2). The styles belonging to these divisions are: (1) Rancho Peludo, Guasare, and Dabajuro; (2a) Capacho and La Mulera and (2b) Cumarebo, Guaraguaro, Punta Arenas, and Playa Guacuco (Fig. 9). The later pottery of the Dutch islands of Aruba, Curaçao, and Bonaire also belongs to the Dabajuroid series (Du Rhy and van Heekeren, 1960).

The data regarding these styles are uneven. We know the earlier, Rancho Peludo and Guasare styles only from Cruxent's 1957 and our 1961 excavations at the Rancho Peludo site, which have already been discussed. Dabajuro, the type style, is based primarily upon test excavations by Osgood and Howard (1943, pp. 128–31, 63–74) in the Maracaibo and Coro areas and upon extensive surface collection by Cruxent around Dabajuro itself. The Capacho and La Mulera sites were excavated by Cruxent in 1956; the Cumarebo style is based upon another surface collection; Guaraguaro, on test excavations by Osgood and Howard (1943, pp. 33–41) and upon various surface collections; Punta Arenas, on excavations by the writers in 1950; and Playa Guacuco, on excavations by Cruxent and Alfredo Boulton in 1949 (Cruxent and Rouse, 1958–59).

The Dabajuroid series has by far the greatest extension in time and space of any Venezuelan series (Fig. 9). According to our Rancho Peludo radiocarbon dates, it began as a local tradition in the Maracaibo basin during the third

EPOCHS	PERIODS	MOUNTAINS	COAST								ISLANDS	PERIODS	DATES
		San Cristobal Area	Maracaibo Area	Coro Area	Tucacas Area	Puerto Cabello Area	La Guaira Area	Río Chico Area	Barcelona Area	Cumaná Area	Porlamar Area		
Indo-Hispanic	V			DABAJURO								V	
Neo-Indian	IV	LA MULERA / CAPACHO	DABAJURO	DABAJURO		CUMAREBO			GUARA-GUAO	PUNTA ARENAS	PLAYA GUACUCO	IV	1500 A.D.
	III		GUASARE									III	1000 A.D.
	II		RANCHO PELUDO									II	300 A.D.
Meso-Indian	I		RANCHO PELUDO									I	1000 B.C.
Paleo-Indian													5000 B.C. 15,000

Fig. 9. Chronology of the Dabajuroid series

millennium B.C. and survived there until historic time, as is indicated by the presence of European trade objects in the latest sites of the Dabajuro style on the Peninsula of Paraguana. (Sherds of the Dabajuro style have also been found at Nueva Cadiz, the first Spanish town in South America, to be discussed in a later chapter, and at the mission site of Santa María Arenales in the Barquisimeto area [Cruxent and Rouse, 1958–59, pp. 71–74].) Thus, the series persisted for four millennia, from Meso-Indian time through the entire Neo-Indian epoch into Indo-Hispanic time. During Period IV of the Neo-Indian epoch it spread from the Maracaibo basin and the Coro area, both parts of the coast, into two of the other four topographic regions of Venezuela, the mountains and the islands offshore. Between its two furthest points, the San Cristobal area in the Andes and Margarita Island in the Porlamar area, it had covered a distance of about 800 miles, following the shoreline.

This geographical distribution is not out of line with the distribution of comparable series in other parts of the New World, e.g., the "horizon styles" of the Central Andes (Bennett and Bird, 1960, Fig. 19), but the temporal distribution is astonishing. It is so great that Rouse was hesitant to accept the original date of 2820 B.C. for Rancho Peludo, the first style in the series, based upon Cruxent's 1957 excavation (Appendix, Y-578). Cruxent, on the contrary, argued that the date was reasonable because the Rancho Peludo style is so much simpler than the subsequent members of the series. It was to settle this difference of opinion that the two of us re-excavated Rancho Peludo in 1961 and obtained a series of 12 additional charcoal samples, six of which have been analyzed by the Yale laboratory (Appendix, Y-1108-I to Y-1110). As we have seen, the two earliest dates which resulted seem to pertain to an earlier, Paleo-Indian occupation of the site, but the other four are consistent with the original, 2820 B.C. date and confirm it (Rouse and Cruxent, 1963). There is still one weakness; we were unable to obtain charcoal samples for the Guasare style, which succeeded that of Rancho Peludo at the site, and so are uncertain whether it dates from late Period II and/or Period III. Until further fieldwork enables us to fill out the sequence of dates, we have tentatively placed the Guasare style in Period III (Fig. 9).

The traits of the original, Rancho Peludo style, which were summarized in the discussion on the Meso-Indian epoch (Chap. 4, D), may be said to characterize the series. In more detail, these include grit temper; construction of the vessel by the coiling method; finish of its lower part with fabric impression or by roughening the surface with fingers (a technique which still survives in the folk pottery of the Andes); perforated annular bases; bowls with incurved sides; ollas, which often have simply banded necks; human heads with appliqué features; and elemental geometric designs in punctation and appliqué work. To them, the Guasare style adds more complex neck bands, which can better be called corrugations, more elaborate punctated and applied designs, incision, and red painted designs. The Dabajuro style also has shell temper, hollow legs and rims occasionally surmounted with lugs, more complex shapes such as bottles with double spouts, several kinds of rod and strap handles, a great variety of geometric and zoomorphic lugs of which the "coffee-bean eye" is typical, and complex painted designs in black and/or red on white (Fig. 10, Pl. 12). The designs include not only straight parallel-line, rectangular, and triangular motifs but also simple curvilinear figures. Frets, ticked lines, and lines bordered with triangles or claviform motives are among the most distinctive features (Fig. 10, D; Pl. 12, C).

The styles of the horizon which was so widespread during Period IV are all like Dabajuro, but in general the farther one goes from the Dabajuro locality, the simpler these styles become. The pottery of the Dutch islands, which are closest to the homeland of the Dabajuro style, is quite complex (Du Rhy and van Heekeren, 1960). In the Andes, too, the Capacho style is fairly well developed, but the subsequent style of La Mulera is simpler in both shape and decoration. The series similarly lost traits as it spread eastward along the coast; for example, the Guaraguaro style lacks perforated annular bases, legs, and hollow rims, as well as three-color painted designs. On the other hand, the Punta Arenas style, even farther east, does have legs and the three-color designs.

The Dabajuroid sites all consist primarily of refuse, those on the coast containing large numbers of shells. Burial is in the refuse or, in the case of most of the western styles,

Fig. 10. Pottery of the Dabajuro style

in urns. There are no structures of any kind or any evidences of religious development, except for an occasional clay figurine in the west. Trapezoidal stone celts are typical, as are metates and manos. Stone amulets and carved stone pestles have been found in association with the Dabajuro style, and shell gouges in association with Guaraguaro.

In our technical monograph (Cruxent and Rouse, 1958–59, p. 257), we suggested that the Dabajuroid series developed "out of a Tocuyanoid background." The discovery of the Rancho Peludo sequence renders this unlikely, since it makes the Dabajuroid series earlier than the Tocuyanoid. We do not know the origin of the earliest, Rancho Peludo style. The development from it into the Guasare style has to be considered a local one, since there is little, if any, evidence for foreign influence. The change from Guasare to Dabajuro, on the other hand, may have been caused by diffusion. Certain traits, such as hollow legs and figurines, are derivable from the Tocuyaroid series, but the painted designs, in particular, point in other directions. Such elements as ticked and straight parallel lines relate Dabajuro on the one hand to the later, Tierroid series of western Venezuela and to the Ocumaroid series of central Venezuela, and on the other hand to the Second Painted horizon of northwestern Colombia (Reichel-Dolmatoff, 1954) and, less closely, to the Chibcha pottery of highland Colombia (Haury and Cubillos, 1953) and to Coclé in Panama (Lothrop, 1942). Frets and lines bordered with triangular or claviform figures also form part of this widespread horizon, though their occurrence is more sporadic. We had best defer discussion of the origin of the horizon until we have considered the other Venezuelan members, i.e., the Tierroid and Ocumaroid series (see Chaps. 6, C and 7, D).

Returning to the problem posed at the beginning of this chapter, we may ask when intensive cultivation of maize began in the Dabajuroid series. The simplest answer would be to say that it arrived with the influences from Colombia and Central America which have just been described, i.e., during Period IV. However, the direction in which these influences traveled—whether to or from Venezuela—is by no means certain; as will be discussed below (Chap. 7, D), it is not unlikely that they diffused from Venezuela to Colombia and perhaps to Central America. Moreover, Period IV is probably too late, since intensive agriculture seems to have been present in the Tocuyanoid series as early as the second half of Period II (see below). We simply do not know when intensive cultivation first appeared in the Dabajuroid series. Perhaps we may learn something about this in the further fieldwork planned at Rancho Peludo, e.g., by obtaining a larger sample of griddles and metates and manos, which will enable us to determine when manioc gave way to maize.

Finally, a few words about the spread of the horizon out of the Maracaibo basin during Period IV. We view this as the result of migration rather than diffusion of ceramic traits, because the series appears relatively pure in all its occurrences and shows very little admixture with local traits. Moreover, the series exerted strong influence on various local styles, notably those of the Ocumaroid series, which will be discussed later.

It is noteworthy that clay griddles, indicative of manioc cultivation, are virtually absent even in the easternmost styles of the Dabajuroid series, though they are common in the nearby sites of the local styles. From this it is inferred that the Dabajuroid people brought maize agriculture with them as they moved east, introducing it into the area of manioc agriculture. This may be considered further evidence that the spread of the series eastward was the result of a migration rather than of diffusion of individual ceramic traits.

B. TOCUYANOID SERIES

The Tocuyanoid series has a much simpler distribution. It consists of only five styles: Tocuyano and Sarare in the Barquisimeto area and Aeródromo in the San Felipe area of the mountains; Agua Blanca in the adjacent Barinas area of the Llanos; and Cerro Machado in the La Guaira area of the coast (Fig. 2). All these styles except Sarare date from the second half of Period II; Sarare is placed in Period III (Fig. 11).

Cruxent noticed the type site of Tocuyano in the spring of 1950 while driving along a highway that had been cut through the site, and we excavated it that very summer. It lay under two meters of sterile soil, which we removed with bulldozers. Since a site of the Tierra de Los Indios style, dating from Period IV, lay on the surface nearby and since the accumulation of two meters of soil prior to the habitation of this site must have taken some time, late Period II does not seem an unreasonable age for the Tocuyano deposit. The age is confirmed by a radiocarbon date of 295 B.C. (Appendix, M-257).

Cerro Machado is the only other style based upon excavation. The site of that name was dug by Cruxent in 1956,

EPOCHS	PERIODS	LLANOS	MOUNTAINS		COAST		PERIODS	DATES
		Barinas Area	Barquisimeto Area	San Felipe Area	Puerto Cabello Area	La Guaira Area		
Indo-Hispanic	V						V	
								1500 A.D.
Neo-Indian	IV						IV	
								1000 A.D.
	III		SARARE				III	
								300 A.D.
	II	AGUA BLANCA	TOCUYANO	AERODROMO		CERRO MACHADO	II	
								1000 B.C.
Meso-Indian	I						I	
								5000 B.C.
Paleo-Indian								15,000

Fig. 11. Chronology of the Tocuyanoid series

when it became apparent that it was about to be destroyed in construction of a residential suburb. The chronological position is based upon seriation within the local area, as well as upon a radiocarbon date of 40 B.C. (Appendix, Y-457). The remaining three styles are known only from surface collections by various people (Cruxent and Rouse, 1958–59).

The sherds obtained at Tocuyano are medium fine textured and grit tempered. Bases are annular, flat, or consist of legs, occasionally resting on rings. The legs are most distinctive: they tend to be hollow, bulbous, and to extend up the side of the vessel almost to the rim (Pl. 13, B). Both bowls and jars are common. They have plain or occasionally hollow rims and their outer surfaces are decorated with complex curvilinear geometric designs, incised or painted red and/or black on a white background (Fig. 12; Pls. 13,

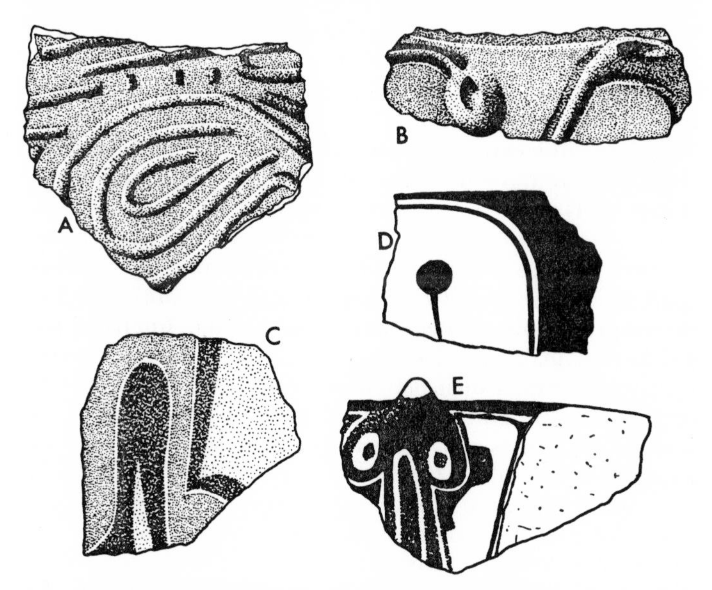

Fig. 12. Pottery of the Tocuyano style

14). Snakes and human faces are also modeled and painted on the vessel wall (Pls. 13–16), but lugs and handles are rare. We obtained very few other artifacts in our limited excavations.

Cerro Machado, Aeródromo, and Agua Blanca are similar to Tocuyano, though not so complex. Sarare, as befits its later chronological position, differs in several respects. It has a new form of vessel with tall, slightly insloping sides, and its designs are painted directly on the clay, without a white slip to form the background.

All the Tocuyanoid sites are places of habitation with the exception of Agua Blanca, which is a burial cave. No human bones were found in the refuse sites, but this means little since the excavations were so brief. Indeed, we know practically nothing about the Tocuyanoid series except its pottery.

Since the Tocuyanoid pottery is complex and highly stylized, it must have had a long history behind it. In our technical monograph we suggested that it may have been derived from the First Painted Horizon in Colombia, which is rather similar and which appears to have been approximately contemporaneous (Reichel-Dolmatoff, 1954). La Pitía, an independent style within the Maracaibo area (Fig. 3), may have been an intermediary between the two (Chap. 6, D).

There are enough differences between the First Painted horizon and La Pitía, on the one hand, and the Tocuyanoid series, on the other, to suggest that they are related by diffusion of traits rather than by migration. Intensive cultivation of maize is, of course, one of the traits (or better, trait complexes) which may have spread, but we cannot be certain of this. The Tocuyano site yielded no metates and manos, yet this is not necessarily significant since our excavation was small. There were manos at Cerro Machado.

At first glance, the Barquisimeto area seems likely to have been the place of origin of the series, since it is near the center of distribution, its Tocuyano style is the most complex, and the Tocuyano site has yielded the older radiocarbon date. However, the series is still so poorly known that these data mean little; it would be premature, for example, to draw conclusions from only two radiocarbon dates (see Chap. 2, C). If the series is derived from the First Painted Horizon and La Pitía, the most probable routes of diffusion would be along the intervening part of the coast, in which case the Tucacas area would be a likely place of origin for the series, since it offers an entrance from the coast into the Barquisimeto area via either the Tocuyo or the Yaracuy valley (Fig. 2). We venture to predict that, when material dating from the second half of

Period II is found in the Tucacas area, it will turn out to belong to the Tocuyanoid series.

C. TIERROID SERIES

The final series of western Venezuela is named after the site and style of Tierra de los Indios in the Barquisimeto area of the mountains (Fig. 2). There are four other styles besides the type: Chipepe, Mirinday, and San Pablo in adjacent parts of the mountains, the Mérida, Trujillo, and

EPOCHS	PERIODS	LLANOS	MOUNTAINS				COAST	PERIODS	DATES
		Barinas Area	Mérida Area	Trujillo Area	Barquisimeto Area	San Felipe Area	Puerto Cabello Area		
Indo-Hispanic	V				TIERRA DE LOS INDIOS	SAN PABLO		V	
Neo-Indian	IV	CAÑO DEL OSO	CHIPEPE	MIRINDAY	TIERRA DE LOS INDIOS	SAN PABLO		IV	1500 A.D.
	III							III	1000 A.D.
	II							II	300 A.D.
Meso-Indian	I							I	1000 B.C.
Paleo-Indian									5000 B.C. 15,000

Fig. 13. Chronology of the Tierroid series

San Felipe areas respectively; and Caño del Oso in the Barinas area of the Llanos. The San Pablo style also extends into the Puerto Cabello area of the coast. Thus, the Tierroid series has the same geographic distribution as the preceding Tocuyanoid series, except that it is in a more westerly part of the coast and extends farther up into the mountains. It is limited in time to Periods IV and V, immediately following the latest style of the Tocuyanoid series (Fig. 13).

The Tierra de los Indios style is known primarily from excavations by Osgood and Howard (1943, pp. 90–91) at the type site and by Brother Nectario María at nearby Guadalupe. Kidder (1944, pp. 91–92) dug at Mirinday and the related site of Los Chaos in 1934 and Cruxent excavated at Mirinday in 1953. Cruxent also tested the type sites of

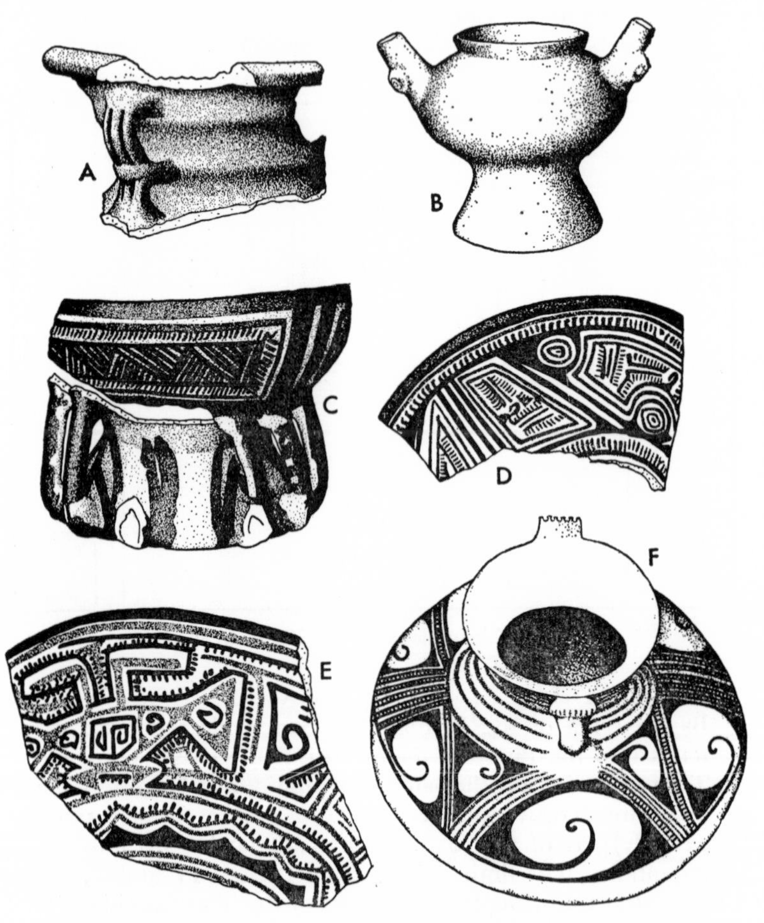

Fig. 14. Pottery of the Tierra de los Indios style

Chipepe and Caño del Oso in 1948 and 1949, respectively. Otherwise, the various styles are based upon surface collections, which are quite extensive, coming from as many as eleven sites in the case of the San Pablo style (Cruxent and Rouse, 1958–59).

The dating of these sites is based upon several different lines of evidence. First, there is the stratigraphy at Tocuyano, to which reference has already been made (Chap. 6, B). Next, we are able to seriate Tocuyano, Sarare, and Tierra de los Indios in the Barquisimeto area, so that the last must be the latest. Third, we have a radiocarbon date of A.D. 1350 for the Mirinday site (Appendix, Y-454). Finally, pottery of the Tierra de los Indios style has been found associated with Spanish artifacts in an Indian burial at Guadalupe and at the Spanish mission sites of Santa María Arenales and San Javier de Agua Culebra. Sherds of the San Pablo style were also found at the latter site (Cruxent and Rouse, 1958–59, pp. 257–58).

While the sherds of the Tierra de los Indios style vary considerably, some are among the best made in Venezuela, thin, fine, and hard. They are tempered with fine sand. There is an occasional neck band, as in the Dabajuroid series, but none of the Dabajuroid roughening of surfaces.

Instead, Tierroid surfaces are smooth and polished. Bowls and jars are common, being frequently provided with legs or annular bases (Fig. 14). The legs do not extend so high up the vessel body as the legs of the Tocuyanoid series; and typically they are surmounted by lugs, as in the Dabajuroid series (Pl. 17). Horizontal rod-like handles are also diagnostic; some rise across the aperture of the vessel. Appliqué work, modeling, and incision receive little emphasis, presumably because they would mar the smooth surfaces of the vessels. Instead, painting is the dominant form of decoration. It is done in various combinations of red, black, and white, though the white background is less common than in either the Dabajuroid or the Tocuyanoid series (Pl. 18). The designs are also less complex; for example, the Dabajuroid frets and lines bordered with claviform figures are lacking (Fig. 14). The spiral is a common motif, and occasionally tiny birds are shown (Pls. 17–19).

Once again, the pottery becomes simpler as one moves away from the type style. The further one goes into the high Andes, i.e., into the Mirinday and Chipepe styles, the coarser the pottery becomes, the simpler the shapes, and the smaller the number of colors in the painted designs. Chipepe, for example, has neither legs nor annular bases and the designs are all painted red on white. The San Pablo and Caño del Oso pottery is also cruder but retains legs, including a distinctive solid form, and has more color combinations than the high Andean styles.

The greater part of the earth and stone constructions of Venezuela are associated with the Tierroid series. These include the causeways and accompanying mounds of the Llanos, which pertain to the Caño del Oso style (Pl. 11, A, B); the shaft graves and rock piles of the high Andes, which are probably to be correlated with the Chipepe style (Pl. 10, D); and the shrine caves, with which the Mirinday style is associated. Tierra de los Indios pottery is also found in mounds, but these may not be intentional. Incense burners, clay and stone figurines, amulets, and bat-wing pendants occur with Mirinday pottery (Pls. 28, 29); and clay figurines are also associated with most of the styles (Fig. 14, G).

There is no mystery about the origin of this series. It almost certainly developed out of the preceding Tocuyanoid series. As we have seen, it also has a number of similarities to the Dabajuroid series, e.g., in its form of legs, the presence of neck bands, and certain painted designs. Whether these traits passed from the Dabajuroid to the Tierroid series or vice versa is uncertain; our chronology is not good enough to determine in which series they first appeared.

This problem is related to another, the question whether the resemblances between the Tierroid, late Dabajuroid, and Ocumaroid series, on the one hand, and the Second Painted horizon, on the other, are due to diffusion from Colombia to Venezuela or from Venezuela to Colombia (see Chap. 6, A). If the latter, then the traits involved probably developed first in the Ocumaroid series, since they occur earliest there (see Chap. 7, D).

D. OTHER STYLES

The majority of the unclassifiable styles occur in the western part of Venezuela, which is probably a reflection of the fact that this part of Venezuela has been less intensively worked than the rest of the country. Two of them are worthy of comment, because they seem to be related in one way or another with the Tocuyanoid series.

La Pitía style. As we have seen (Chap. 6, B), La Pitía provides a possible connecting link between the Tocuyanoid series and the First Painted horizon of northeastern Colombia. It is known almost entirely from the type site, a single large shell heap on the Peninsula of Guajira north of the city of Maracaibo (Fig. 2). The site came to light in 1953 when road crews began to remove shells from it for use in highway construction. Attracted by news of this, Professors Miguel Acosta Saignes and Barbosa de la Torre, of the Universidad Central and the Universidad de Zulia, respectively, collected pottery after the bulldozers in 1953, and Cruxent did the same in 1954. Patrick Gallagher (1962) undertook extensive excavations in the remnants of the shell heap in 1960, while a graduate student at Yale University. Since he has not yet worked up his material, the following remarks are based primarily upon the previous work at the site.

The material is so variable that it must cover a long span of time and, presumably, several successive styles, which it

Fig. 15. Pottery of the La Pitía style

is expected that Gallagher will unravel. Meanwhile, we must treat the entire collection as a unit; we are unable even to separate out the material at the base of the deposit, which has been discussed in connection with the earlier, Meso-Indian epoch (Chap. 4, E). The pottery shares many traits with the Tocuyanoid series and with Dabajuroid pottery. Therefore, we extend the present undivided style from late Period I into IV (Fig. 3). Gallagher has obtained a single radiocarbon date, of 10 B.C., for the lower part of the refuse (Appendix, Y-855).

It is the similarities with the Tocuyanoid series which have attracted the most attention. These include hollow legs, curvilinear broad-line incision, red-and-black-on-white painting, and a distinctive comb-like motive (Fig. 15). But La Pitía shares these same traits with the First Painted Horizon as well, and has additional resemblances with the latter, e.g., black incised ware and female figurines. Hence, it has to be considered closer to the Colombian pottery than to the Tocuyanoid series.

The First Painted horizon is limited to northeastern Colombia. Nothing like it is known from northwestern Colombia, but there is similar polychrome pottery—including, e.g., the comb-like motive—in Panama, Costa Rica, and the rest of Central America, extending up into the Maya area. Because the radiocarbon dates for this pottery in Central America are ca. A.D. 200, several centuries later than the earliest Venezuelan dates, Coe (1962, pp. 176–77) has theorized that polychrome pottery diffused from south to north, beginning in western Venezuela and ending in Meso-America. On the other hand, in our technical monograph (Cruxent and Rouse, 1958, vol. 1, p. 248), we assumed diffusion in the opposite direction, from Colombia into Venezuela. Possibly the pottery originated in Colombia or Panama and spread in both directions.

If polychrome pottery did diffuse from Colombia to the Tocuyanoid series via La Pitía, the question may be raised why this did not also affect the Dabajuroid series. Rancho Peludo, the early Dabajuroid site, is less than 50 km. from La Pitía. We can only say that this is not the first time we have encountered two or more styles existing side by side in the same area with little evidence of mutual influence (e.g., see Fig. 3). It may be suggested that at this time the Dabajuroid series was primarily limited to the interior and that the Colombian influences, if they existed, passed along the coast.

Santa Ana style. Material collected from the caves of

Fig. 16. Pottery of the Santa Ana style

Cuchillo and Santo Domingo in the Trujillo area pertains to another style, which is of interest because it has traits reminiscent of both the Tocuyanoid and Barrancoid series, i.e., both western and central Venezuelan pottery. Legs and the painting are Tocuyanoid, while a series of modeled-incised lugs and figures on vessel walls are Barrancoid (Fig.

16). A figurine seated on a stool recalls Colombian pottery (Pl. 25).

It is not possible to do much with these resemblances. The material is from burial caves and therefore perhaps atypical. Its age is unknown. We mention the resemblances here only because they seem to be worth following up. As will be noted in Chapter 7, A, Willey (1958, p. 372) has suggested that the Barrancoid series had its origin in the earliest, Meso-Indian pottery of Panama and Colombia, but he was unable to cite any connecting link between Colombia and central Venezuela, the homeland of the Barrancoid series. The Santa Ana style would provide such a link, if it or an antecedent could be shown to have extended back into the Meso-Indian epoch.

Miscellaneous artifacts. In Plates 21–24 and 26–30, we illustrate a miscellaneous series of artifacts of pottery, stone, and other materials. These are intended to show the artistic range of western Venezuelan artifacts and do not, at least for the moment, have much significance for the culture history of Venezuela. Only one style, Betijoque, has been recognized, and it cannot be adequately dated. Presumably, it was a local development in the states of Trujillo and Lara, possibly out of the Tocuyanoid series.

With two exceptions, the other artifacts illustrated in these plates come from burial caves and are a part of the ceremonial complex characteristic of the Venezuelan Andes. The two exceptions are the resin and the gold figures in Plate 30, A, B. The gold figure is unique and may best be regarded as an importation from Colombia, but the resin figure is distinctively Venezuelan, several other examples having been found on the Llanos.

Chapter 7

NEO-INDIAN EPOCH: CENTRAL VENEZUELA

We turn now to the central part of the country, to the islands of Los Roques, the coast from the Tucacas area to the Río Chico area, the mountains from the Valencia basin to the Caracas basin, and the San Fernando and Valle de la Pascua areas on the Llanos (Fig. 2). This region has roughly the shape of an inverted triangle, reaching down to the point where the Río Apure flows into the great bend of the Orinoco River. The river itself, from Apure south to the Puerto Ayacucho area, may also belong in the central division, but is beyond the scope of this book.

The geography of central Venezuela is such that the northwestern corner of the triangle occupies a key position. This is the place where the mountains, trending northeastward from western Venezuela, reach the shore and turn eastward to become the coastal range. Just past the turn, they enclose the fertile basin of Lake Valencia, which was a center of population and agriculture in Neo-Indian time, as it is today. From the Valencia basin to the Puerto Cabello area of the coast is only a short distance and the two areas show many evidences of mutual influence during Neo-Indian time.

The Puerto Cabello area also lies at the end of an even

easier, though longer, descent from the western mountains via the Yaracuy valley, and here, too, there are evidences of influence, such as the intrusion of the Tocuyanoid series (Chap. 6, B). When one adds to this the possibility of contacts east and west along the coast and with the islands offshore, as evidenced by the spread of the Dabajuroid series (Chap. 6, A), one can understand why the situation in the Puerto Cabello area is the most complex in Venezuela. We have had to distinguish four more or less contemporaneous styles there during Period IV alone (Cruxent and Rouse, 1958–59, Fig. 26).

The southern part of the triangle, the San Fernando area, is also important because it is the place where three possible routes of diffusion come together, one down the Orinoco River from Amazonia, the second down the Apure River from the Andes, and the third down the Portuguesa and Pao Rivers from the Valencia basin. The last is the route through which the waters of Lake Valencia spilled over into the Orinoco during Period III, as discussed at the beginning of Chapter 5.

Diffusion in the directions indicated has given central Venezuela an unusually varied Neo-Indian culture, partaking of both western and eastern developments. We have been able to distinguish four local series—more than in either the west or the east—and in addition all of the western series extend into the region.

A. BARRANCOID SERIES

Since the Barrancoid series consists of two groups of styles, one in central and the other in eastern Venezuela, we could equally well discuss it in connection with either region. Our earliest dates for it are in the east, but it seems to have been intrusive there and so we discuss it in the chapter on central Venezuela.

There are three styles in the central part of the series, La Cabrera, El Palito, and Taborda, the first in the Valencia basin of the mountains and the other two in the adjacent Puerto Cabello area on the coast; and two styles in the east, Barrancas and Los Barrancos on the lower Orinoco

River (Fig. 2). Los Barrancos developed into a third style, Guarguapo, which might also have been included here, since it preserves many Barrancoid traits, were it not for the fact that it has more traits of the Arauquinoid series, which apparently diffused downstream to it from the middle Orinoco valley (Chap. 7, B). Even so, we will discuss the work done on the Guarguapo style and its chronology here, since they are intimately related to our research on the local Barrancoid styles.

Professor Mario del Castillo was the first to investigate a site of the Barrancoid series when he dug at Los Tamarindos, type site for the La Cabrera style, in 1930–32. He was followed in 1933–34 by Alfred Kidder II (1944), who made extensive stratigraphic excavations at Los Tamarindos. In 1945, Antonio Requena, Walter Dupouy, and Cruxent undertook similar stratigraphic excavations of even greater scope at El Palito and Trompis, sites of the El Palito style on the coast (see Chap. 2, A). Cruxent and his students in the Universidad Central followed this up in 1957 with excavations at two other sites of the El Palito style, Aserradero and Playa Ocumare. The other coastal style, Taborda, is known only from a test excavation made by Cruxent at the type site in 1957.

Osgood and Howard (1943) initiated excavation of the eastern part of the series by digging at Los Barrancos, type site for the style of that name, in 1941. We encountered the entire eastern sequence of styles in our 1950 excavations at the site of Saladero. The same year, we also made a test in the town of Barrancas itself, which is the type site for the style of that name. We returned in 1955, to collect another radiocarbon sample from the site of Saladero, and again in 1957, when we worked at Guarguapo, type site for the style of that name.

During the course of our various trips to the Barrancas area we also made a survey of the surrounding region, which is of interest because it indicates that the population expanded steadily. We know of only five sites in which Barrancas-style pottery is predominant, including one at Puerto Ordaz, the iron-loading installation some distance up the

Orinoco. Los Barrancos-style pottery was obtained in appreciable numbers at nine sites, including one at Tucupida within the delta itself; and Guarguapo-style pottery, at thirteen sites (Cruxent and Rouse, 1958–59, pp. 223–33).

Los Tamarindos is the key to the chronology of the central group of styles. Here, Kidder (1944, pp. 31–36) found two series of strata, a lower one consisting of sand and gravel that had evidently been laid down by the lake as it rose to its maximum level, during Period III (see above,

EPOCHS	PERIODS	COAST — Puerto Cabello Area	MOUNTAINS — Valencia Area	CENTRAL AND EASTERN LLANOS	ORINOCO — Barrancas Area	PERIODS	DATES
Indo-Hispanic	V					V	
Neo-Indian	IV	TABORDA				IV	1500 A.D.
	III	EL PALITO	LA CABRERA		LOS BARRANCOS	III	1000 A.D.
	II	EL PALITO	LA CABRERA		BARRANCAS	II	300 A.D.
Meso-Indian	I					I	1000 B.C.
Paleo-Indian							5000 B.C. 15,000

Fig. 17. Chronology of the Barrancoid series

Chap. 5), and an upper one composed mainly of humus formed after the lake had fallen again, during Period IV. The lower stratum contained pottery of the La Cabrera style and the upper one, pottery of the Valencia style, in accordance with the chronology shown in Figure 17.

The El Palito style is synchronized with La Cabrera because the two are so much alike; and this is confirmed by two radiocarbon dates of A.D. 260 and 290 for the Aserradero site (Appendix, Y-579, Y-580). We assume that both styles began earlier, during the latter part of Period II, because of the presence at El Palito of Saladoid trade sherds, some decorated with crosshatched designs which, as we shall see (Chaps. 7, F; 8, A), are markers for that subperiod. The El Palito site also yielded trade sherds from the Los Barrancos style on the lower Orinoco River, the Ocumare style in the local area, as well as Aroa and a Dabajuroid style to the west, all of which agree with the chronology given in Figure 17. We place the Taborda style in Period IV partially because it is strongly influenced by other styles of that period and partially because of the presence of a trade sherd from the Valencia style.

The Orinocan subseries is based mainly on the sequence obtained by us at the Saladero site. As will be noted later (Chap. 8, A), we encountered refuse of the earlier, Saladero style in thin, localized deposits at the bottom of this site. Barrancas-, Los Barrancos-, and Guarguapo-style potsherds became successively dominant in the much thicker overlying stratum (Cruxent and Rouse, 1958–59, Tables 9–12). We have obtained five valid radiocarbon dates for these styles, as follows (a sixth sample had become contaminated; see Appendix):

Barrancas style: 985, 955, and 930 B.C. (Appendix, Y-40, Y-316, Y-294)
Los Barrancos style: A.D. 510 (Appendix, Y-499)
Guarguapo style: A.D. 1640 (Appendix, Y-38-39)

These confirm the stratigraphy within the upper part of the site, but not succession of the Saladero style and Barrancoid pottery, for the Barrancas-style dates overlap those for the Saladero style, which range from 1010 to 700 B.C. (Appendix, Y-42 to Y-44). Nevertheless, we place Saladero in the first quarter of Period II and Barrancas in the second quarter (cf. Figs. 28 and 17) because stratigraphy must be given priority over radiocarbon dates, other conditions being equal (Chap. 2, C). Various occurrences of trade sherds, which confirm the chronology by providing evidence of the contemporaneity of Barrancoid and other styles, need not be detailed here.

Logically, we should begin to describe the pottery with the Central Venezuelan styles, since the series is more likely to be indigenous to that part of the country. Being later, however, the central Venezuelan styles show more influences from other series, and therefore a better impression of the Barrancoid series can be obtained by beginning with its Orinocan members.

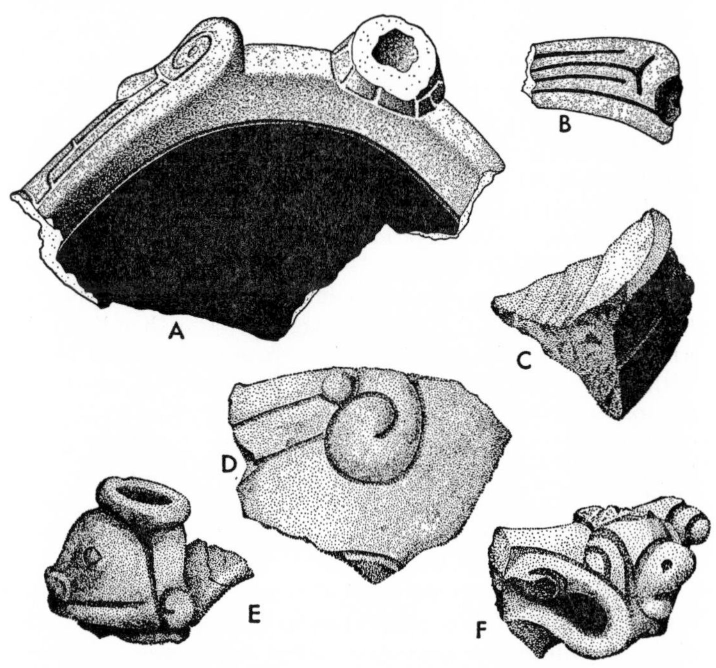

Fig. 18. Pottery of the Barrancas style

The sherds of the Barrancas style are unusually thick, heavy, and coarse, though their surfaces are smooth and fine. They always have grit temper, and come typically from bowls with short, solid, annular bases, vertical sides, and flanges extending horizontally outwards from the rim (Fig. 18). Bottles with double spouts connected by strap handles are not uncommon (Pl. 31, B). Some vessels appear to have been even larger than the Dabajuroid burial urns but, so far as is known, they were not used for burial. Instead, they may have served as containers for beer (*chicha*) during festivals, as reported by the first explorers of the Orinoco valley (Alvarado, 1945, pp. 138–39).

Barrancas decoration is characterized by a combination of modeling and incision, either on vessel walls, flanges, spouts, or lugs. Walls are occasionally decorated with large human faces (Pl. 32, B), but more often both walls and flanges bear geometric figures, such as dimples, spirals, and limb- or foot-like motifs (Fig. 18, D). The lugs and the figures on spouts are typically prismatic in shape and portray human or animal heads. Doughnut-shaped eyes and nostrils incised with circles or spirals are diagnostic (Pl. 33, B). Other figures are simply incised on the vessel wall with an occasional punctation; these are bold and relatively simple (Fig. 18, B).

Barrancas pottery also has a few features that can be attributed to Saladoid influence: vertical strap handles (Pl. 31, C); red, black, or yellow slip, covering areas outlined with incised lines (Fig. 18, A); and, more rarely, white-on-red painted designs (which are on Barrancas-style sherds, so they cannot be considered trade ware). Both the strap handles and the white-on-red painted designs appear out of place for, as on Saladoid pottery, they are on a relatively small scale, which contrasts strongly with the bold, massive, overall appearance of the rest of the decoration.

The Los Barrancos pottery lacks most of these Saladoid traits, as if the Barrancoid potters had reverted to the style of decoration most congenial to them. The pottery is somewhat thinner and finer than in the previous Barrancas period and its surfaces are more highly polished, sometimes only in restricted areas (Pl. 33). Blackware is commoner. The double-spouted vessels disappear. Head lugs, incised designs on the vessel wall, and modeled-incised figures on the wall all become more complex (Pls. 32, A; 33; 34; 35, B). A new technique of excision—cutting out areas of the vessel surface—makes its appearance; and lines more frequently end in dots. Overall, the designs give more of an appearance of intricacy, interest in detail, and stylization, which contrasts markedly with the boldness, simplicity, and massiveness of the Barrancas designs. Los Barrancos is the classic pottery of the series.

Insofar as the Guarguapo style is Barrancoid, it may be regarded as a degeneration from the classic pottery. Its modeling and incision are simpler, sloppier, and less stylized, as if the potters had lost interest in the traditional designs. For the most part, they had apparently turned to traits of a new series, Arauquinoid (Chap. 7, B).

The La Cabrera pottery, of the Valencia basin, is generally like the Orinocan material, especially in its modeled-incised heads, which occur on lugs, spouts, and in this case also on clay pipes (Pl. 36, B). On the other hand, La Cabrera lacks the complicated modeled-incised and incised designs of the Orinoco (Pl. 31, A), and it has a number of western and southern traits, notably perforated annular bases, rod handles, rectilinear incised and punctated designs, and appliqué ridges, frequently decorated with punctations. These suggest a trend in the direction of the subsequent Valencia style (Chap. 7, C).

El Palito pottery, on the coast, is very similar to La Cabrera pottery, especially in its lugs and in the presence of pipes of clay (Pl. 35, A), but it also has several additional features: incised tabular lugs, corrugated rims, and legs. These may be attributed to diffusion along the coast, the first from Río Guapo and the Saladoid series (Chaps. 7, F; 8, A) and the other from the nearby Ocumaroid series (Chap. 7, D). The Taborda style shows even stronger influence from the Ocumaroid series, notably painted designs, as is to be expected from its longer period of contact.

The excavations in Barrancoid sites have been extensive enough to yield a relatively great variety of other kinds of artifacts, of which only a part can be mentioned here. Fragments of griddles are everywhere abundant, but there are no metates except for one specimen from El Palito. Pot rests are also common. Spindle whorls of clay have been found on the Orinoco, and stone pestles, at El Palito (Pl. 36, A). La Cabrera has yielded a bone flute carved with

Barrancoid designs (Pl. 38, A). Bone points of Manicuaroid types were associated with the Orinocan styles.

The complexity of Barrancoid decoration is such as to suggest some sort of ceremonial development, but there is little evidence of this. All sites consist simply of refuse, and burial is directly in the refuse, ordinarily without any grave objects. Figurines are the exception; we know of only one, despite the great amount of digging and collecting that has been done (Pl. 37). Only La Cabrera and El Palito have yielded amulets, and these are rare. The La Cabrera and El Palito pipes, of course, can be regarded as ceremonial objects, and they are more common.

In our technical monograph (Cruxent and Rouse, 1958–59, p. 247), we assumed that the Orinocan part of the series had given rise to the central Venezuelan segment because the Orinocan was earlier. However, we failed to take into consideration the fact, which became apparent only after our subsequent work on the Peninsula of Paria, that the Barrancoid series is intrusive into the Orinoco valley (Fig. 31). We must therefore seek another source for the series.

There are two possibilities: (1) the series may have diffused in the opposite direction, from the Valencia basin to the lower Orinoco River; or (2) it may have spread to both areas from a third place, most probably the San Fernando area of the central Llanos, whence there are good routes of diffusion, up the Portuguesa and Pao Rivers into the Valencia basin and down the Apure and Orinoco Rivers past Ronquín to Barrancas (Fig. 2). We are inclined to favor alternative (2), primarily because the later styles of the San Fernando area have more elaborate modeling and incision than is present in the Valencia basin (see Chap. 7, B), but both regions need to be searched for material dating from the first half of Period II that would shed light on this problem. For the moment, we have only the occurrence of Barrancoid trade sherds in the Meso-Indian sites of the Pedro Garcia complex, which suggests that Barrancoid people were somewhere on the Llanos about 500 B.C. (Chap. 5, C).

We must also search for still earlier material, dating from

the Meso-Indian epoch (Period I), in order to determine the ultimate origin of the series. When we first excavated the material, we were impressed with its resemblances to the Chavin horizon style of Peru (e.g., Cruxent, 1951, pp. 151–53), but the work done in Amazonia since then has yielded no sign of a connecting link between the two as early as the Meso-Indian epoch. Willey (1958, p. 372) has suggested that the Barrancoid series may be derived from the earliest, Meso-Indian pottery of Colombia and Panama, which is also incised and in some cases modeled—e.g., the pottery of Barlovento and Puerto Hormiga of Colombia and Monagrillo of Panama. This is now a more reasonable hypothesis—especially in view of the fact that Reichel-Dolmatoff (1961, p. 354) has recently obtained a radiocarbon date of 2913 B.C. for Puerto Hormiga—but proof will be lacking unless and until we find similar Meso-Indian pottery in Venezuela (Chap. 6, E).

Turning to the history of the Barrancoid series after it has reached the Valencia basin and the lower Orinoco River, we are on firmer ground. The series clearly spread from the Valencia basin to the Puerto Cabello area on the coast, for it is intrusive there (see Chap. 7, D). In the basin, it gave way to the Valencia style at the close of Period III, but persisted on the coast during Period IV as the Taborda style.

On the lower Orinoco, as we have seen, the Los Barrancos style developed at the close of Period III into the Guarguapo style, which is more Arauquinoid than Barrancoid, reflecting influences from upstream. Meanwhile, during Period III or earlier, the series had spread into British Guiana, where it gave rise to a new style or series of styles, to which Evans and Meggers (1960) have given the name Mabaruma. It also spread during the latter part of Period III to Trinidad, where it is known as the Erin style (Rouse, 1953b).

In our technical monograph (Cruxent and Rouse, 1958–59, p. 30), we noted that certain Barrancoid traits likewise spread out to the Greater Antilles during Period III and were partially responsible for the rise of a new series (Chicoid) in that area during Period IV (op. cit., Fig. 4). We may now state more specifically, as a result of the analysis to be presented in the next chapter (8, A), that these were traits which the Saladoid people had acquired from the Barrancoid series while still on the mainland and then carried to the islands. In other words, there was no direct contact between the Barrancoid and Chicoid series; by the time the latter had begun to spread throughout the Greater Antilles, the Barrancoid series had become extinct on the Orinoco.

B. ARAUQUINOID SERIES

Four styles comprise the Araquinoid series: Arauquín and Matraquero, near San Fernando in the central Llanos; Camoruco, which is around Parmana on the middle Orinoco River; and Guarguapo, at Barrancas on the lower Orinoco (Fig. 2). The first two are known only from surface collections, made by Vincenzo Petrullo (1939) in 1934 and by local inhabitants in 1956–57. The rest have been thoroughly excavated, the Camoruco style by Howard (1943) in 1941 and Guarguapo by the writers in 1950 and 1957.

The Camoruco and Guarguapo excavations are discussed in connection with the Saladoid and Barrancoid series respectively, since they have yielded primarily material of those series (Chap. 8, A, and above). Here, we need only repeat that refuse of the Camoruco style ("late Ronquín" in Howard, 1943) overlay a much thicker deposit of Ronquín style refuse at the site of the latter name, while Guarguapo pottery overlay that of the Los Barrancos style at the sites of Saladero and Guarguapo. Since Ronquín and Los Barrancos both date from Period III, we are able to place Camoruco and Guarguapo in Period IV (Fig. 19). Guarguapo is extended into Period V because of the presence of European trade sherds and a radiocarbon date of A.D. 1640 (Appendix, Y-38-39).

The Arauquín and Matraquero styles are likewise placed in Period IV, but only because of their stylistic resemblances to Camoruco and Ronquín and also to Valencia, the Period IV style of the Valencia basin (see the following section). Arauquín also has lugs like those of the Los Barrancos style, which leads us to extend the Arauquín style back into the second half of Period III, making it the earliest of the Arauquinoid styles (Fig. 19). Presumably, it is the source of the few Arauquinoid sherds that have been found associated with the Ronquín and Los Barrancos styles, and with the Cotua style up the river (see Chap. 8, A).

EPOCHS	PERIODS	LLANOS: San Fernando Area	ORINOCO: Parmana Area	ORINOCO: Barrancas Area	PERIODS	DATES
Indo-Hispanic	V			GUARGUAPO	V	
						1500 A.D.
Neo-Indian	IV	ARAUQUIN; MATRAQUERO	CAMORUCO	GUARGUAPO	IV	
						1000 A.D.
	III	ARAUQUIN			III	
						300 A.D.
	II				II	
						1000 B.C.
Meso-Indian	I				I	
						5000 B.C.
Paleo-Indian						15,000

Fig. 19. Chronology of the Arauquinoid series

Still further upstream, beyond the region under consideration in the present volume, the Nericagua "phase" of Evans, Meggers, and Cruxent (1959) bears a relationship to the Arauquinoid series, but the exact nature of this relationship will not be known until the Nericagua material has been studied in greater detail. Here, we can only note that ten radiocarbon dates have been obtained for Nericagua, ranging between A.D. 650 and 1390 (Appendix, P-160 to P-262). These agree well with our placement of the Arauquinoid series in Periods III and IV.

The pottery of the Arauquinoid series is easy to distinguish because it is tempered with spicules of fresh-water sponges, which may be seen in the sherds under a strong

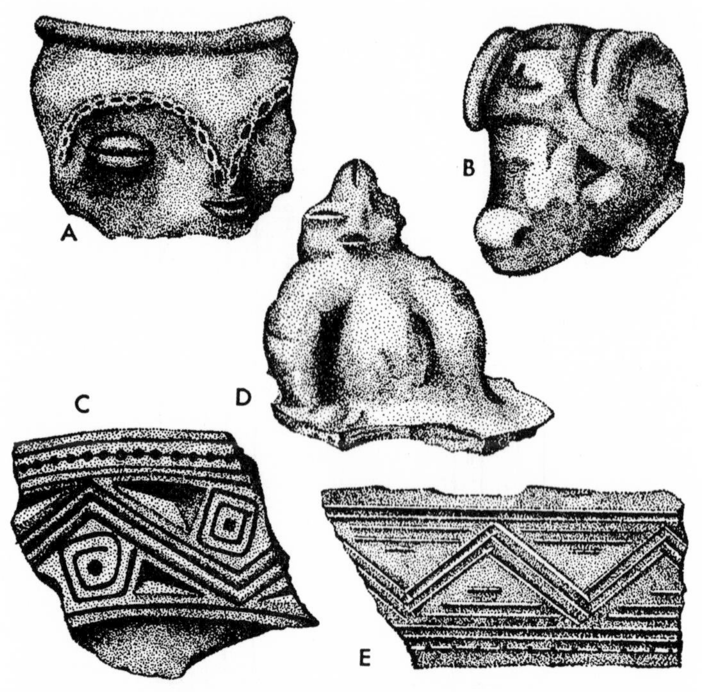

Fig. 20. Pottery of the Arauquín style

magnifying glass. These give it a characteristic grey color and make it soft to the touch. Globular, collared jars or bottles, with human faces in appliqué work on the collars, are also typical. These faces have arching eyebrows and coffee-bean eyes, as in western Venezuela (Fig. 20, A). In addition, there are bowls with outsloping sides, which are frequently provided with a broad bevel inside the rim bearing incised designs (Fig. 20, E). These recall the Barrancoid pottery of eastern Venezuela, though they are more sharply and deeply incised.

The designs vary from style to style. Basically, they consist of parallel lines inclined in alternate directions and bordered at the top and bottom with horizontal lines. In the Arauquín style, there are curving as well as straight lines and the designs are quite complex. The spaces between motifs are frequently excised, less often punctated (Fig. 20, C). The Matraquero designs are simpler and the areas between lines tend to be filled with punctations rather than excision. Camoruco is similar, but completely lacks curved lines and has almost no excision. Guarguapo designs are the simplest and crudest of all.

The bowls of all styles are decorated with lugs. Typically, these have appliqué features like the faces on collars, including coffee-bean eyes. The Arauquín style also has modeled-incised head lugs in the Barrancoid tradition, with doughnut-shaped rather than coffee-bean eyes (Fig. 20, B, D). Guarguapo pottery is provided with similar lugs, more elaborately done, and with modeled-incised designs on the vessel wall. All of the styles, finally, also have appliqué ridges on the wall, which are frequently punctuated. Painting is nonexistent, except for a few red-slipped sherds in the Arauquín style.

The nature of the Arauquín sites is not known. The Matraquero sites are reported to be *medanos* or mounds of earth which the Indians constructed to raise the level of their dwellings above the flood waters. These are a necessity in the Llanos Bajos, where there is more flooding than in the high plains to the north. The site of Camoruco, on the middle Orinoco, also consists of a mound, set some distance back from the river. Otherwise, however, the Indians of the middle and lower Orinoco River lived on the higher sections of the river bank itself, which become islands while the river is in flood. Burial customs are unreported.

Fragments of clay griddles are common in all collections except that of Petrullo, who may not have bothered to collect them. Cylindrical clay stamps are known from

Arauquín, Matraquero, and Camoruco, and figurines from the first two. Pot rests and spindle whorls of clay are also widespread. There are also a few celts, hammers, hammer-grinders, and metates and manos.

Since the Arauquín style is the earliest, according to present knowledge, the other styles may have developed from it, i.e., the series may have diffused down the Orinoco. The increasing simplicity of the styles as one moves downstream favors such a conclusion, as does the fact that the Arauquínoid series replaced the Saladoid and Barrancoid series in the middle and lower parts of the valley respectively. The series may have been carried into the middle Orinoco valley by a migration, for the Ronquín and Camaruco styles are separated by a sharp break. Conversely, the spread to the lower valley must be a matter of diffusion, since the Guarguapo style retains so many traits of the previous Los Barrancos style as to make it difficult to decide whether to classify it in the Araquinoid or Barrancoid series.

As for the origin of the series, we tentatively suggest that it developed in the San Fernando area or along the great bend in the Orinoco River out of an as yet undiscovered Barrancoid style. Such a style would also serve to account for the origin of the Barrancoid series (see above, A).

If this theory is correct, the practice of incising bevels inside the rims of Arauquinoid pottery may be said to have developed from the practice of incising the flanges of Barrancoid pottery, by a process of omitting the flanges and dropping the designs down inside the rim of the vessel. The modeled-incised head lugs of the Arauquín style would also be derived from this postulated Barrancoid predecessor.

On the other hand, the designs themselves and the technique of excision which was sometimes used to make them are not Barrancoid. Possibly the designs were derived from the rectilinear painted decoration of the Tierroid and Memoid series to the west and the north.

The collared jars decorated with human faces and the other appliqué work must have had a different origin.

They are widespread in Colombia, and we have elsewhere suggested that they diffused down the Meta River from that country (Cruxent and Rouse, 1958–59, p. 38). They may have been accompanied by the practice of making clay stamps (Pl. 38, B), if not by figurines and other western traits such as the ball game and the cultivation of maize, which were practiced by the Otomi Indians of the San Fernando region in historic time (Rouse, 1954).

Meggers and Evans (1961, Fig. 6) have concluded that many of the decorative features just discussed spread out from the Arauquinoid series in two directions: (1) downstream to the latest pottery of their Mabaruma phase in British Guiana; and (2) up the Orinoco River to the Nericagua phase and thence down into the lower part of the Amazon basin, e.g., to the well-known Santarem style at the mouth of the Río Tapajós. They apply the phrase "Incised-punctated horizon style" to this spread. Linné (1925, p. 53), however, has postulated a reverse diffusion of sponge-spicule tempering from the lower Amazon, and we would not exclude the possibility that other traits of the Arauquinoid series may also have spread from Amazonia into the Orinoco basin.

C. VALENCIOID SERIES

This series is named after the style, basin, and lake of Valencia in the central mountains (Fig. 2). It also includes the styles of Las Minas and El Pinar, in the vicinity of Los Teques and Caracas, respectively; the Topo and Río Chico styles, around La Guaira and Río Chico in the adjacent parts of the coast; and the Krasky style, on the Los Roques Islands off the coast of the La Guaira area. There is likewise a Cementerio Tucacas style in the Tucacas area further west along the coast. The series begins at the close of Period III and extends through Period IV into V (Fig. 21).

Valencia pottery has become the best known in Venezuela as a result of the pioneer excavations by Ernst, Marcano, Oramas, Jahn, R. Requena, Bennett, Osgood, and Kidder, which have been discussed in an earlier chapter (2, A). Most of these men dug in the mounds of La Mata, at the eastern end of the lake of Valencia, but Kidder worked at the Los Tamarindos site on the Peninsula de la Cabrera. Cruxent has also tested various sites of the Valencia style; most recently, in 1958, he obtained the mateiral for two radiocarbon analyses from a La Mata mound. Altogether, thirteen sites of the style have been investigated (Cruxent and Rouse, 1958–59, pp. 169–71).

The Topo style is the next best known, a large number of its sites having been surveyed by Oramas in the 1930's

EPOCHS	PERIODS	COAST		MOUNTAINS			COAST		ISLANDS	PERIODS	DATES
		Tucacas Area	Puerto Cabello Area	Valencia Area	Los Teques Area	Caracas Area	La Guaira Area	Río Chico Area	Los Roques Area		
Indo-Hispanic	V									V	1500 A.D.
Neo-Indian	IV	CEMENTERIO TUCACAS		VALENCIA	LAS MINAS	EL PINAR	TOPO	RIO CHICO	KRASKY	IV	1000 A.D.
	III									III	300 A.D.
	II									II	1000 B.C.
Meso-Indian	I									I	5000 B.C.
Paleo-Indian	--									--	15,000

Fig. 21. Chronology of the Valencioid series

and by Cruxent and Dupouy in the 1940's. The Las Minas style is based upon test excavations in three sites, the first two by Dupouy and Cruxent in 1944 and the third by Cruxent in 1955. The Río Chico style was excavated by Acosta Saignes, de Armas Chitty, and Cruxent in 1949; and the Krasky style by Pedro Jam and Alberto Méndez, of the Sociedad de Ciencias Naturales La Salle, in 1950. The Cementerio Tucacas and El Pinar pottery, finally, have been mainly obtained in connection with the construction of roads and houses (Cruxent and Rouse, 1958–59).

The main basis for putting the Valencia style in Period IV is the stratigraphy encountered by Kidder in his excavations at Los Tamarindos, where Valencia refuse overlay that of the La Cabrera style (Kidder calls it a "phase") of Periods II–III (see above, A). Kidder was also able to correlate his Valencia stratum with the fall in the level of Lake Valencia after it had reached its maximum height during Period III. Further confirmation is provided by three radiocarbon dates of A.D. 920, 940, and 920 (Appendix, Y-630 to Y-632). These are slightly earlier than the beginning of Period IV but not early enough to justify extending the Valencia style back into Period III. The style is carried forward into Period V because of the presence of two Valencia-like sherds in the Spanish town of Nueva Cadiz.

We date the Topo style in Period IV because it seriates at the end of the sequence in the La Guaira area, and in Period V because a Spanish trade sherd was found in one of its sites. The remaining styles are put in Period IV solely on account of their typological resemblances to the Valencia and Topo styles.

The Valencia pottery is coarse, tempered with sand and mica, and rather rough surfaced. The vessels tend to be simple globular bowls or ollas. The bowls sometimes have perforated annular bases; the ollas are frequently surmounted by collars decorated with human faces (Pls. 39, 40). These are delineated in appliqué work, as in the Arauquinoid series, and they have similar coffee-bean eyes and high, arching foreheads. Human arms, hands, and simple vertical ridges are also applied to the vessel wall; occasionally these are punctuated (Pl. 40, A). Small rod handles and minute-featured lugs in the form of animals or of human heads are diagnostic of the style (Fig. 22, A–G; Pl. 39, D). The human heads tend to be broad, flat, and canoe-shaped and they, too, have coffee-bean eyes. Incision consists primarily of straight parallel lines inclined in opposite directions and separated by punctations. There is no painting, except for an overall red slip.

The remaining styles are linked to the Valencia pottery by their material and shapes (though they lack the collar) and especially by their lugs. None of them has either the Valencia faces or its incision. In the Topo style, on the other hand, there are corrugations and red-and-black-on-

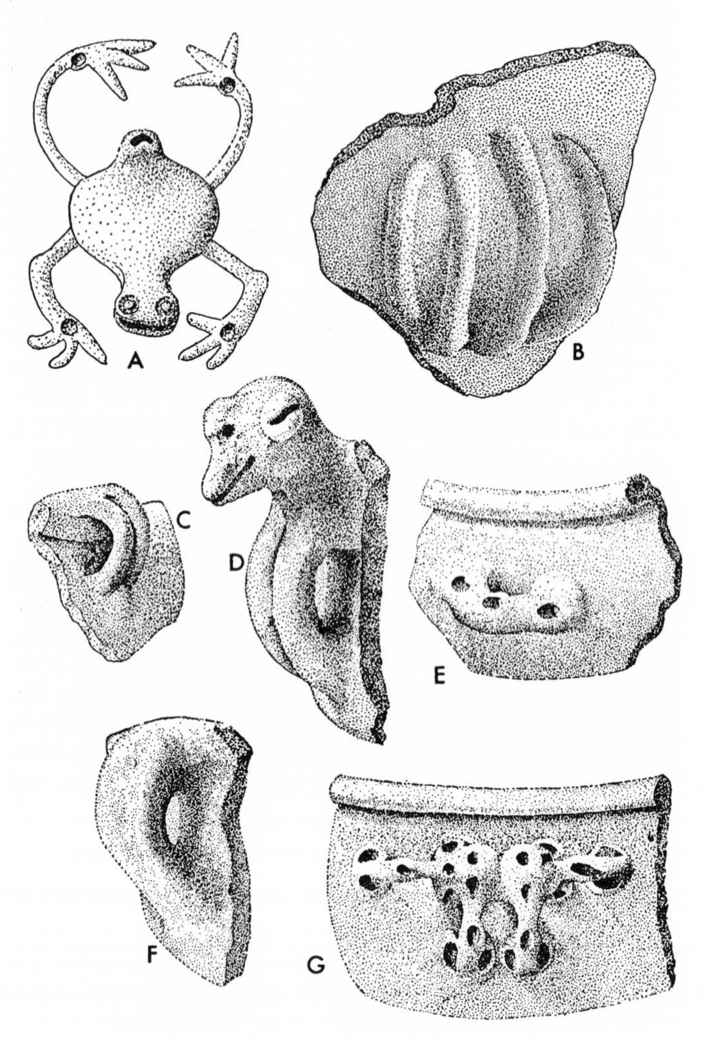

Fig. 22. Pottery of the Valencia style

white painting, which may be attributed to either Dabajuroid or Ocumaroid influence.

Bennett (1937) obtained evidence in his excavation of a La Mata mound that the Indians first lived there in pile dwellings, placed over the water. Subsequently they brought in earth to provide a dry base for their houses and their refuse accumulated on this base, completing the construction of the mound. Osgood (1943, p. 43) concluded that the mound he dug was originally built for burial purposes, but that the Indians subsequently lived upon it and deposited their refuse there because its top was above the level of the floodwaters. Mounds like this do not occur in associa-

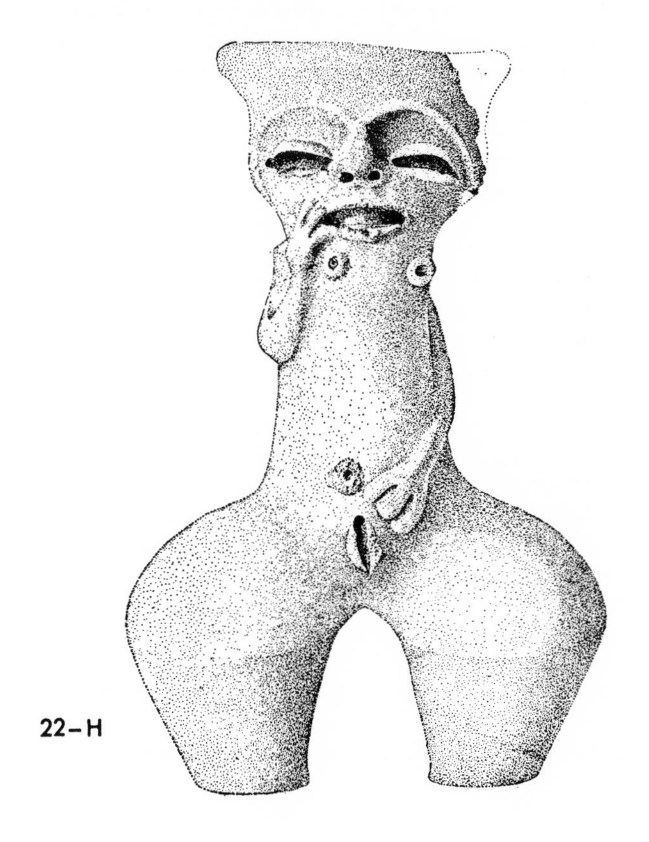

22–H

tion with the other styles of the series. Urn burial, though, is common, not only in the Valencia mounds but also in the Las Minas and Río Chico styles.

The clay figurines of the Valencia style are well known. Most portray women, either standing or sitting, but there are also some animals (Frontispiece; Fig. 22, H; Pls. 41–44). They have the same kinds of appliqué features as the lugs, and the women have similar canoe-shaped heads. They also resemble the faces on vessel collars in their coffee-bean eyes and arched eyebrows. None of the other styles has figurines, except possibly Topo.

Griddles abound in all the sites. A clay pipe (Pl. 45), miniature clay stool, manos and metates, polishing stones, rectangular and bat-wing pendants of stone, and shell beads, rings, and pendants are among the other objects reported from the Valencia mounds. (A shell pendant is illustrated in Pl. 46, A.) The Topo sites have yielded stone and shell celts; stone hammers, metates, manos, and mortars; beads of stone and shell; and stone pendants. Presumably, therefore, the Valencioid people practiced both manioc and maize agriculture.

The series may best be regarded as a local development within the Valencia basin. A number of features of the previous La Cabrera style foreshadow this development, e.g., perforated annular bases, rectilinear incised and punctated designs, and appliqué ridges. Beyond this, the series must have been strongly influenced by the Arauquinoid pottery of the Llanos, with which it shares such traits as collars, faces with coffee-bean eyes and arching eyebrows, and the minute lugs with pinched features. The poor finish of the sherds is also more reminiscent of the Arauquinoid series than of the rest of the pottery in western and north-central Venezuela, where the prevalence of painting led the potters to devote some attention to smoothing the vessel surfaces. Construction of mounds is another trait which may have spread northward from the south central Llanos to the Valencia basin, presumably via the Portuguesa and Pao Rivers; we have seen that it was widespread in the

Llanos Bajos as a means of raising houses above the floods which covered that area during the rainy seasons.

The Valencioid series contrasts sharply with the other late series of western and north-central Venezuela, i.e., the Dabajuroid, Memoid, Ocumaroid, and Tierroid series. It is the only one of them without corrugations, for example; the only one without painted designs of any kind; and the only one except the Memoid which lacks legs. On the other hand, its figurines, the miniature stool, and the stone and shell amulets associated with the Valencia style do link it with western Venezuela. So also does the presence of urn burial.

The series reached its highest development in the Valencia basin and became simpler as it spread from there. Whether there was a movement of people or simply diffusion of ceramic traits is unclear. A migration is indicated only in the case of the Topo style, by the fact that its sites are all on the slopes of the sierras, some distance from the shore, whereas the previous Cerro Machado and Boca Tacagua people had lived close to the shore. This suggests a movement of people out of the Caracas basin and down into the La Guaira area. As we have seen, the Topo people were influenced in various ways by the coastal ceramic traditions.

D. OCUMAROID SERIES

This series is limited to three areas of the coast: Tucacas, Puerto Cabello, and La Guaira (Fig. 2). It consists of only four styles: Aroa in the first area; Ocumare and Palmasola in the second; and Boca Tacagua in the third. The series begins in Period III and ends in IV (Fig. 23).

The series first came to light when the writers collected pottery at Boca Tacagua in 1946. Cruxent subsequently excavated there, encountering four burials in the shell refuse. In 1952, he dug at the Aroa site, with the assistance of Miguel Schön and Pedro Jam; and in 1956–57, at Ocumare with the help, during 1957, of students from the Universidad Central. The fourth style, Palmasola, is known only from surface collections, also made by Cruxent in 1954 (Cruxent and Rouse, 1958–59).

The chronology of the Ocumaroid series is the weakest of all. None of its styles has been found in stratigraphic position, nor do we have any radiocarbon dates for them. We have been forced to rely upon two indirect lines of

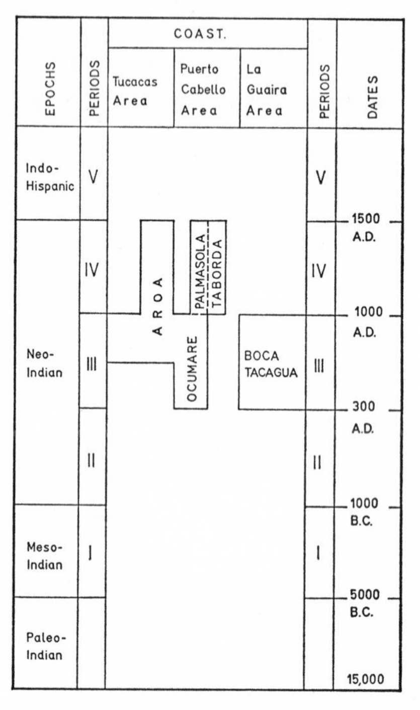

Fig. 23. Chronology of the Ocumaroid series

evidence: (1) seriation of the styles in the La Guaira area and (2) synchronization by means of trade sherds, of which there are fortunately an appreciable number because of the coexistence of so many styles in the Puerto Cabello area. For example, sherds of the Ocumare style have been found in excavations of El Palito (Barrancoid) sites and conversely two El Palito pipes were obtained at Ocumare, thus establishing the contemporaneity of those two styles. Since El Palito is dated by the radiocarbon method around the beginning of Period III, we may assign the same relative date to the Ocumare style.

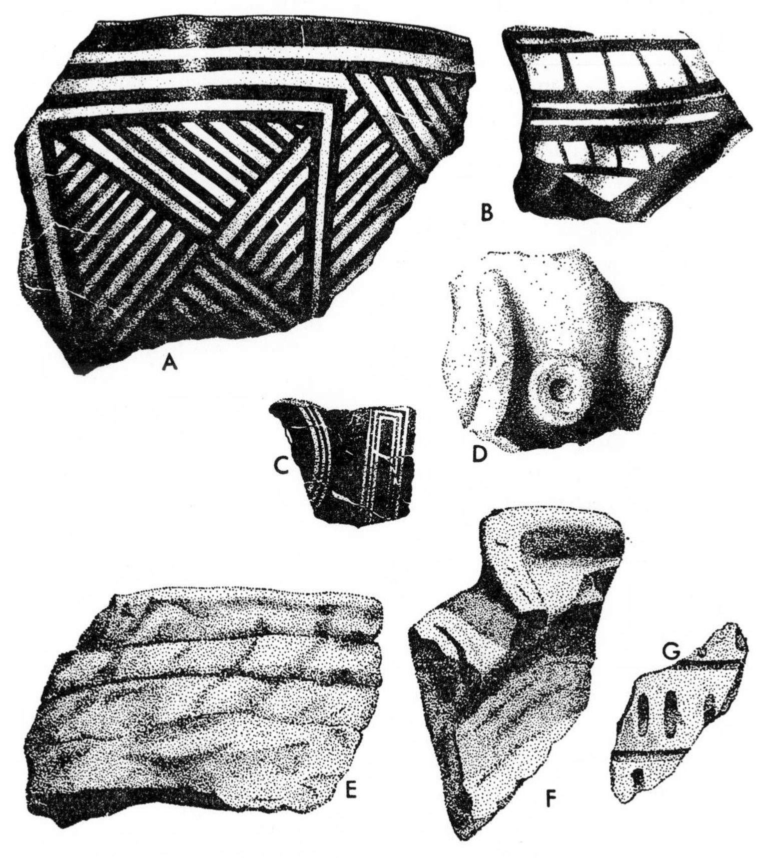

Fig. 24. Pottery of the Ocumare style

The potsherds of this style are medium fine textured, thick, and contain grit temper. Ollas and globular bowls are common. They frequently have annular or perforated annular bases, or less commonly legs, as in western Venezuela. The absence of handles and the dominance of painting in red and black on white also point to the west, possibly to the Tocuyanoid series, though the designs emphasize straight parallel lines, triangles, and ladder-like figures, contrary to the curvilinear designs of the Tocuyanoid series (Fig. 24, A–C). Corrugation of the outer surface of the vessel beneath the rim is another typically western trait (Fig. 24, E). On the other hand, there are also a few local traits, including rim flanges, incision, and simply modeled lugs (Fig. 24, D, F, G). These may be derived from the Barrancoid series, which was also present in the local area.

The Aroa style, further west, has essentially the same characteristics, with the addition of fabric impression, another western trait, and vertical strap handles, an eastern trait. Boca Tacagua, on the other side of Ocumare, has more resemblances to the east, as befits its position. These include triangular rims, flanges, vertical strap handles, and red painting, which is areal rather than lineal. All of these suggest Saladoid influence (Chap. 8, A). On the other hand, the dominant form of painting is that typical of the rest of the Ocumaroid series. The presence of ticked lines is perhaps worth noting, because these are so widespread in western Venezuela.

The final style, Palmasola, which succeeds Ocumare in the Puerto Cabello area during Period IV, again shows more resemblances to the west, probably reflecting the spread of the Dabajuroid series eastward at that time. A number of Dabajuroid traits make their appearance, including fabric impression, horizontal rod handles, and lugs with coffee-bean eyes.

All the sites contain shell refuse. The only burials encountered were four placed directly in the refuse at Boca Tacagua. Clay griddles were common in all sites except the westernmost, Aroa, a fact which indicates that manioc agriculture was characteristic of the series, despite the ceramic resemblances to the west.

The Ocumaroid series may best be interpreted as a local development whose course was shaped by the various influences which have been noted. But were the Ocumaroid people basically westerners who adopted eastern traits, or were they easterners influenced from the west? We incline toward the former alternative, both because Ocumaroid pottery is fundamentally western and, more important, because its sites are distinct from those of the Barrancoid series, even though the two are contemporaneous within the Puerto Cabello area. The latter fact indicates that the Ocumaroid series cannot be derived from the Barrancoid series, and that, therefore, the latter must be intrusive into the Puerto Cabello area.

As we have seen (Chap. 6, B), the western, Tocuyanoid series was in the La Guaira region, if not in the rest of central Venezuela, before the Barrancoid series. We suggest that the Ocumaroid series developed out of this earlier Tocuyanoid occupation as a result of influences not only from the Barrancoid but also from the Saladoid series. The former may well have been responsible for the introduction of manioc cultivation, but the latter is more likely to have stimulated the development of the typical Ocumaroid painted decoration, since it, too, included painting whereas the Barrancoid series did not.

It must not be forgotten, however, that the Ocumaroid series shared the general trends in painted decoration which prevailed in western Venezuela during Period IV, such as an emphasis on parallel lines and a tendency toward angularity. These trends were less highly developed in the Ocumaroid series than in the Dabajuroid or Tierroid. (A single fret design in the Palmasola style is the exception; Cruxent and Rouse, 1958–59, Fig. 56: 16.) Nevertheless, the trends appear earlier in the Ocumaroid series, so far as our present evidence goes, and so may have originated there. If so, the Ocumaroid series is responsible for a form of decoration which spread throughout western Venezuela, on into the Second Painted horizon of northwestern Colombia and possibly beyond (see Chap. 6, A, C).

E. MEMOID SERIES

The Memoid series has an even more limited distribution than the Ocumaroid, being known at present only in the

Memo and Guaribe styles of the Valle de la Pascua area of the Llanos and the La América style of the Río Chico area, where the Llanos terminate in the coast (Fig. 2). It extends from Period IV into V (Fig. 25).

EPOCHS	PERIODS	LLANOS: Valle de la Pascua Area		COAST: Río Chico Area	PERIODS	DATES
Indo-Hispanic	V	MEMO	GUARIBE	LA AMERICA	V	1500 A.D.
Neo-Indian	IV	MEMO	GUARIBE		IV	1000 A.D.
	III				III	300 A.D.
	II				II	1000 B.C.
Meso-Indian	I				I	5000 B.C.
Paleo-Indian						15,000

Fig. 25. Chronology of the Memoid series

We owe the discovery of the Memo series to the expansion of highway construction in the Llanos after World War II. The site of Memo, for example, became known as the result of construction of a highway bridge across the Río Memo in 1947. The highway engineers called in Cruxent, who excavated extensively. In 1948 he discovered and dug the site of Guaribe in the town of the same name and collected extensively in another site of the same style, Aserradero. In 1955 the two of us obtained additional material from these two sites and also collected at three others which contain pottery of the Guaribe style. The La América style, finally, is known only from an old collection in the Museo de Ciencias Naturales in Caracas (Cruxent and Rouse, 1958–59).

The Memo and Guaribe styles are placed in Period IV, primarily because of their resemblances to the Tierroid and Dabajuroid series, and in Period V, because Memo sherds have been found at the Spanish town of Nueva

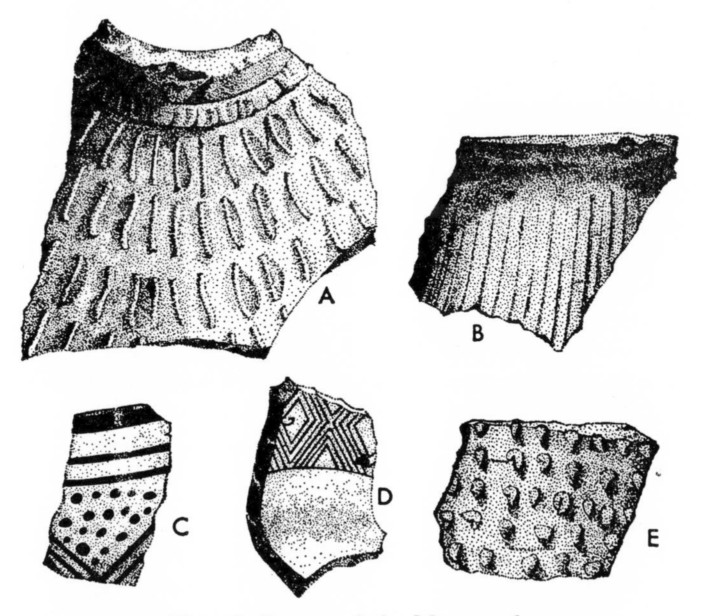

Fig. 26. Pottery of the Memo style

Cadiz (Chap. 9, A). That the two styles are contemporaneous is indicated by the presence of Memo sherds in Guaribe sites and vice versa. The La América collection is placed in Period V because of the presence of Spanish pottery.

Memo sherds are thin, fine textured, and sand tempered. They come from simple globular vessels, typically with flat bases and plain rims. Some sherds are decorated with ridges or dots of clay, applied to their surfaces; the surfaces of others have been roughened by incision, scoring, or punctation; and still others are decorated with painted designs in red (or, rarely, black) on white (Fig. 26). The designs consist of thin parallel lines arranged in triangles or diamonds much like some of the Ocumare designs (cf. Fig. 24). There are only a few plain lugs.

Guaribe sherds are thicker and coarser. Vessel shapes are the same but appliqué work and painting are lacking from the decoration. Roughening of the surface is more elaborate than in the Memo style, including corrugation, fabric impression, and impression of the fingers in addition to scoring and punctation. The La América collection is included in the Memoid series mainly because it has the typical appliqué work.

So far as is known, the sites are all simply places of habitation. Fragments of clay griddles are common in all of them. Other artifacts include celts, hammers, grinders, and a bead of stone; a large quantity of stone chips; a clay stamp; a bone awl; and a shell bead.

The Memoid series is the Llanos equivalent of the Ocumaroid series on the coast. Like the latter, its pottery is mainly western, resembling the Tierroid series in its painting and the Dabajuroid series in its roughening of surfaces; but its agriculture, on the contrary, is of the eastern type and its lack of ceremonial paraphernalia also relates it to the east. It may, therefore, have originated in the same way as the Ocumaroid series, i.e., out of the Tocuyanoid series, which was represented on the central Llanos as well as on the central coast by the Agua Blanca style (Fig. 11).

F. RÍO GUAPO STYLE

A style known as Río Guapo precedes the Río Chico style, of the Valencioid series, in the part of the coast east of Caracas (Fig. 2). It is known from a single site, a deposit exposed in the bank of the Río Guapo at a depth of 4.5 meters. This deposit is difficult to investigate, since it is covered by the river except when the level is lowest at the end of the dry season. Professor Miguel Acosta Saignes, of the Universidad Central, and Cruxent dug a trench there in 1949, and Cruxent returned in 1960 to collect a charcoal sample for radiocarbon analysis.

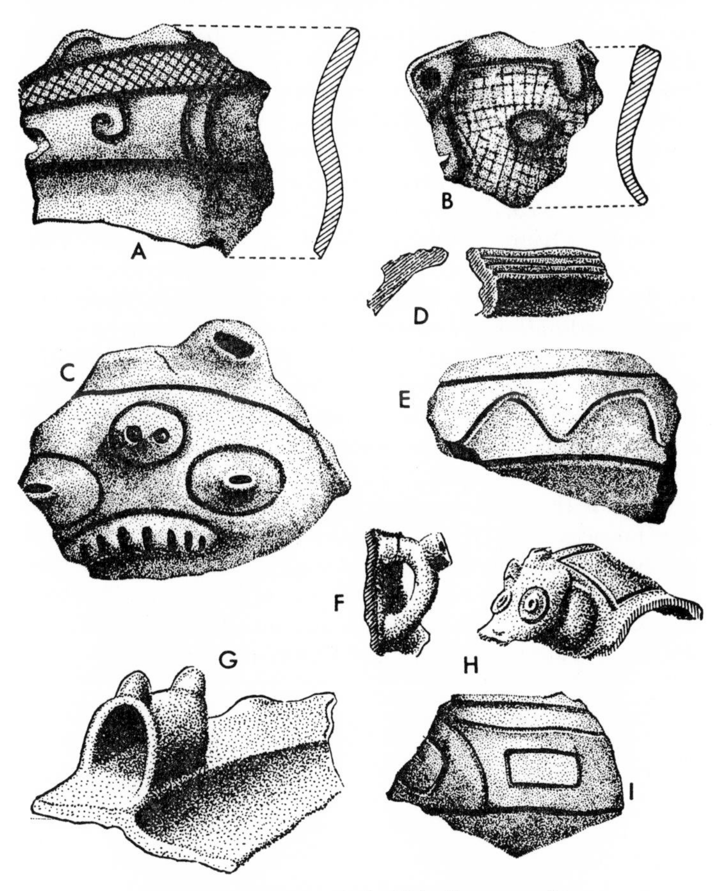

Fig. 27. Pottery of the Río Guapo style

Río Guapo attracts attention because it is the only style in central Venezuela which is closely related to the Saladoid series of eastern Venezuela (Chap. 8, A). It resembles the latter in its fine grit temper, its bell-shaped bowls, thin flanges, vertical strap handles, hollow-backed modeled-incised lugs, tabular lugs, and simple incised designs, which typically include finely crosshatched areas (Fig. 27). Indeed, the only reason the Río Guapo style is not included in the Saladoid series is that it lacks the painting which is diagnostic for that series.

Before analysis of the radiocarbon sample, we had been uncertain whether to consider Río Guapo ancestral to, or an offshoot from, the Saladoid series. The radiocarbon date suggests the latter, for it is A.D. 270, more than a millennium later than the earliest members of the Saladoid series, which are on the Orinoco River (Appendix, Y-1230). In our opinion, Río Guapo must now be regarded as a by-product of an expansion of the Saladoid series westward along the coast shortly after the time of Christ (Chap. 8, A).

As already noted, the Río Guapo style may be responsible for certain trade objects which have been recovered from the Barrancoid sites of the central coast. Indeed, the effect of its trade may have extended even farther westward, since a few zoned, crosshatch-incised sherds have been found at the top of the Meso-Indian shell heap of Cerro Iguanas in the Tucacas area (Rouse, Cruxent, and Wagner, MS) and on the island of Aruba in the Dutch West Indies (Du Rhy and van Heekeren, 1960, pp. 88–89). It is also possible that the Río Guapo style served to transmit Saladoid traits to the Boca Tacagua style of the Ocumaroid series.

Chapter 8

NEO-INDIAN EPOCH: EASTERN VENEZUELA

Eastern Venezuela comprises the islands of the Porlamar area, the coast from the Barcelona area eastward to the mouth of the Orinoco River, the eastern mountains and Llanos, and the middle and lower parts of the Orinoco valley, from the Parmana area eastward to the delta of the Orinoco River (Fig. 2). The region is shaped like a trapezoid, its shorter, top side being formed by the eastern islands and coast and its longer, bottom side by the middle and lower parts of the Orinoco valley. These are the only important sections; the mountains, the Llanos, and the swamps of the Gulf of Paria and the Orinoco delta were poorly inhabited, according to our present evidence.

During the early part of the epoch, as we have seen (Chaps. 4, B; 5, C), Meso-Indians still occupied the islands and the coast, whereas Neo-Indians had already made an appearance on the Orinoco River. Gradually the Neo-Indians encroached on the Meso-Indians until they had overwhelmed them, so that in historic time the latter survived only in the least favorable places (an example is the survival of the Warrau Indians in the delta of the Orinoco River). The following survey of the Neo-Indian series will document this process of encroachment.

We do not know the origin of the Neo-Indian culture but tentatively assume that it developed *in situ* out of the as yet undiscovered ceramic cultures of the Meso-Indian epoch which were postulated in Chapter 4, E. The domestication of manioc is presumed to have been an important part of the process of development, in accordance with Sauer's theory. Unfortunately, by the time we pick up the development, pottery is already at the peak of its perfection, technically speaking, and manioc has already become the basic food of the area, to judge from the large number of clay griddles for cooking it that have been found in the sites. The earlier stages of the development constitute the greatest gap in our knowledge of Venezuelan archaeology at the present time.

A. SALADOID SERIES

Since Rouse's original purpose in coming to Venezuela was to investigate the sources of the Neo-Indian culture of the Antilles and since the Saladoid series is the key to that problem, we have worked more with the Saladoid series than with any other and know more about it. We are now able to distinguish seven styles in Venezuela: Cotua, Ronquín, and Saladero itself on the Orinoco River; Irapa, El Mayal, and Chuare on the coast; and El Agua on Margarita Island (Fig. 2). In addition, the series extends out into the West Indies through the Cedros and Palo Seco styles of Trinidad and a number of as yet poorly defined styles in the Lesser Antilles to the Hacienda Grande and Cuevas styles of Puerto Rico (Cruxent and Rouse, 1958–59, Fig. 4).

Theodoor de Booy (1916) must be credited with the discovery of the series in his excavation at Guire Guire on Margarita Island in 1915. Howard (1943) dug it in purer form at Ronquín in the middle Orinoco valley in 1941. Otherwise, all the excavations have been done by the writers and their associates.

Saladero is considered to be the type site and style because the series is the earliest and purest there, so far as we can tell. We made extensive excavations in this site, near

Barrancas on the lower Orinoco River, in 1950. Moving up the river, we know the Ronquín style from Howard's excavation already mentioned, which was even larger than ours at Saladero, and from small surface collections at other sites (Riley and Olvey, 1960). The Cotua style, in the Puerto Ayacucho area at the head of navigation, is based only upon potsherds collected by Cruxent in the late 1940's (Cruxent and Rouse, 1958–59).

Turning in the other direction to the Güiria area on the Peninsula of Paria, we should note that Cruxent collected pottery from a highway excavation at Irapa in 1951. Realizing that this might be a key region in the distribution of the series, we tried to do further work there in 1955, but were unable to go far enough onto the peninsula because of high water in the rivers that had to be forded. We returned again in 1961, accompanied by Maruja Rolando de Roche, and discovered and excavated six additional sites of the Irapa style (Rouse, Cruxent, and Wagner, MS).

El Mayal, the earlier style in the Carúpano area, further west along the coast, is known from our excavations at the El Mayal 2 site in 1955 and from excavations by Erika Wagner and Cruxent at La Cucaracha in 1960 (op. cit.). Chuare, the later style in that area, was encountered by us in excavations at El Mayal 1 in 1955 and at El Mayal 4 and 6 in 1957. Finally, El Agua, the westernmost style, on Margarita Island in the Porlamar area, is known from de Booy's excavation at Guire Guire, from work by Cruxent and Alfredo Boulton at the same site in 1948, and from a trench which Cruxent dug in El Agua, the type site, around 1950.

The chronology of the Saladoid series is well established, both by stratigraphy and by radiocarbon dating (Fig. 28). Refuse of the type style underlies that of the entire local part of the Barrancoid series at the type site; the Ronquín component is beneath that of the local member of the Arauquinoid series at the site of Ronquín, and the Irapa style was found in the lower stratum at the Cabrantica site on the Peninsula of Paria, underlying a local style named after that site. On the island of Trinidad, too, a combination of stratigraphic study and seriation have demonstrated that a pair of Saladoid styles, Cedros and Palo Seco, are earlier than a Barrancoid style, Erin (Rouse, 1953b).

As for radiocarbon analyses, the Saladero style is dated 1010, 830, and 700 B.C.; El Mayal, A.D. 100 and 300; Irapa, A.D. 220, 325, and 570; and Chuare, A.D. 550 (Appendix, Y-42 to Y-44; Y-297, Y-1230; Y-290, Y-1112, Y-1113; and Y-300). These dates, combined with the stratigraphy and with certain typological trends, to be discussed below, have

EPOCHS	PERIODS	ORINOCO			COAST		ISLANDS	PERIODS	DATES
		Puerto Ayacucho Area	Parmana Area	Barrancas Area	Güiria Area	Carúpano Area	Porlamar Area		
Indo-Hispanic	V							V	1500 A.D.
Neo-Indian	IV							IV	1000 A.D.
	III	COTUA	RONQUIN		IRAPA	CHUARE	EL AGUA	III	300 A.D.
	II		RONQUIN	SALADERO	IRAPA	EL MAYAL		II	1000 B.C.
Meso Indian	I							I	5000 B.C.
Paleo-Indian									15,000

Fig. 28. Chronology of the Saladoid series

led us to place the Saladero style within the first half of Period II; El Mayal and Irapa, in the second half of Period II, with Irapa extending into Period III; and Chuare, in Period III. The remaining styles have been cross-dated with these as shown in Figure 28.

This chronology substantiates the theory (already presented in Chap. 5, C) that the Saladoid people were gradually moving down the Orinoco River to the coast and out onto the islands during the latter half of Period II and the first half of Period III, encroaching upon the previous Meso-Indian inhabitants as they went, in that the styles become progressively later as one moves downstream to the coast and islands. Two additional stratigraphic facts may also be cited in favor of the theory. First, refuse of the Chuare style was found on top of refuse of the Carúpano complex, a member of the Manicuaroid series, at the site of El Mayal 1; and second, a few Saladoid sherds occurred in the refuse of the Punta Gorda complex, the latest in the Manicuaroid series, on the island of Cubagua (Chap. 5, C). It would seem that, after the Saladoid people had reached the coast during the latter part of Period II, they traded pottery to the few surviving Manicuaroid people on the nearby islands, who did not know how to make it themselves (cf. Figs. 28 and 6).

What caused the Saladoid people to move out to the coast? The entrance of the Barrancoid people into the lower Orinoco valley may have had something to do with it, as a comparison of Figures 17 and 28 will indicate. If these chronologies are correct, people of the Saladoid style occupied both the middle and lower parts of the Orinoco valley during the first quarter of Period II. During the second quarter, Barrancoid people seized the lower part of the valley from them. It may be supposed that the Barrancoid newcomers pushed the Saladoid people out through the delta of the Orinoco River to Trinidad and the Peninsula of Paria, thereby initiating the latter's encroachment upon the Meso-Indians of the coast and islands. Unfortunately, our Trinidad and Paria excavations did not carry us far enough back in time to check this supposition (Fig. 28).

In any event, it is clear that the Barrancoid invasion split the Saladoid series into two parts, one in the middle Orinoco valley, which subsequently spread upstream to Cotua, and the other on the coast and islands, which expanded west as far as Margarita Island and north as far as Puerto Rico. These two survived intact through the last half of Period II and all of Period III before giving way to other series—the Arauquinoid on the middle Orinoco and the

Guayabitoid on the coast and adjacent islands (Fig. 28).

Let us turn now to the typological characteristics of the series. Sherds of the Saladero style are easy to distinguish from the pottery of the later Barrancoid styles on the lower Orinoco because they are so thin and fine. They contain

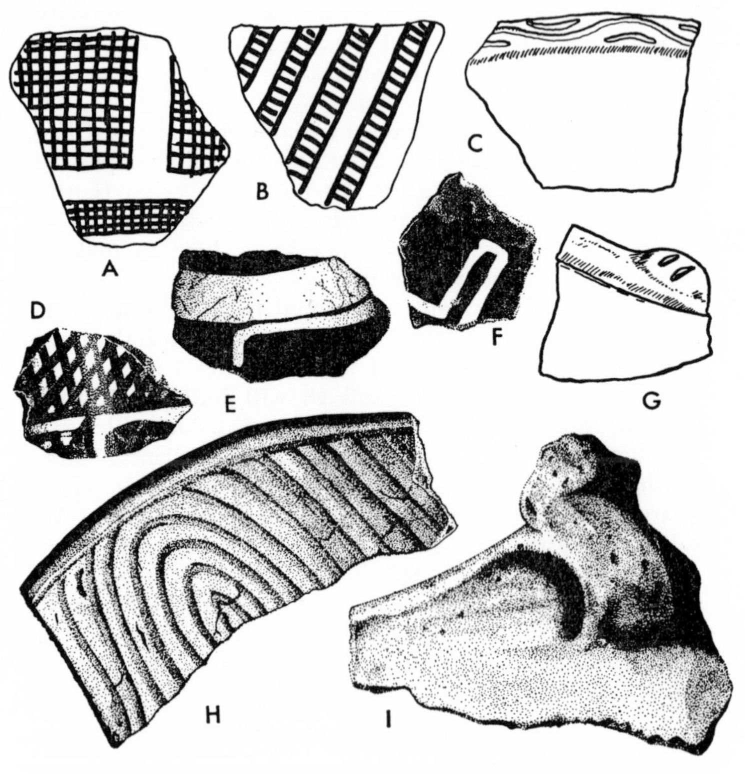

Fig. 29. Pottery of the Saladero style

sparse grit temper and come primarily from wide-mouthed bowls with flat bases. The sides of these vessels tend to curve out gracefully in the form of an everted bell. Rims are plain or beveled but never flanged. There are many vertical strap handles, some surmounted by crude knobbed lugs (Fig. 29, I). Simple tabular lugs also occur on the rim (Fig. 29, G). True modeling, however, is absent, as are punctation and incision, except for a few simple designs composed of arched parallel lines (Fig. 29, C, H). Painting is the most distinctive feature of the decoration. It is done either in red on a plain background or, more commonly, in white on a red background (Fig. 29, A, B, D–F). The red designs consist primarily of crosshatching and the white-on-red designs, of curved areas bordered by thin lines. In some cases, white and red areas have been juxtaposed to produce designs, instead of the former being placed on the latter. Some designs, too, have been produced by rubbing out red paint to expose the plain clay as a background.

In reporting on his excavations at Ronquín on the middle Orinoco, Howard (1943) treated all of his Saladoid pottery as a single unit (which he called "Early Ronquín" to distinguish it from the overlying Arauquinoid pottery). Our findings led us to re-examine his conclusion. We made a cursory survey of a part of his collection—this needs to be confirmed, if possible, by more detailed study—and found that the pottery from the bottommost levels is very much like our Saladero pottery but that it diverges as one goes up through the levels. The sherds become thicker and coarser. Flanges are added to the rims, modeled-incised lugs make their appearance, incised designs become more complex, and punctations are added. All these are traits of the Barrancoid series—though the manner in which they are carried out on Ronquín pottery is not always the same—and they indicate that the Ronquín people had now come under the influence of the Barrancoid intruders in the lower Orinoco valley.

The coastal part of the Saladoid series shows a similar trend: the later the pottery, the more Barrancoid traits it has. For example, the earlier pottery of the Irapa and El Mayal styles lacks flanges, whereas the later pottery of these styles has them, as does the Chuare and El Agua pottery. Lugs are cruder and incised designs less complex in the earlier styles than in the later (cf. Fig. 30 with Pl. 46, B). Incised designs are spread out over the vessel walls in the case of the earlier styles, whereas they tend to be crowded onto flanges in the later ones. Finally, the sherds of the earlier styles are finer and better made than those of the later styles, though this is not necessarily due to Barrancoid influence. All of these changes correspond to trends we have noted in the Ronquín style on the middle Orinoco, and they apply to the Cotua style on the upper Orinoco as well.

In passing, it should perhaps be noted that Evans and Meggers (1962, Fig. 3) have tentatively grouped the Cotua style with their Nericagua pottery from still farther up the Orinoco and with various forms of Amazonian pottery in an "Incised-rim horizon style." We cannot agree with this grouping, since only Cotua, of all the styles mentioned, has such Saladoid traits as white-on-red painting and incised designs on flanges. Evans and Meggers have apparently confused the Cotua style with some potsherds of an Arauquinoid style which also occurred at the Cotua site; it is the Arauquinoid rather than the Cotua style which is related to their "Incised-rim horizon style."

Returning to the nature of the Saladoid series, we have found that the coastal styles have certain traits which are not present on the Orinoco River and which cannot be derived from the Barrancoid series. These include a simply modeled-incised form of head lug with hollow back and a new type of incision, in which certain zones of the vessel surface are crosshatched by means of fine-line incision, in sharp contrast to the broad-line incision of the Barrancoid series (Fig. 30; Pl. 47, E, F).

The origin of these traits is uncertain. Two possibilities may be suggested:

1. The traits may have diffused eastward along the coast into the Saladoid series. This possibility is indicated by the fact that both traits are characteristic of Río Guapo, a non-Saladoid, non-Barrancoid style in the Río Chico area of the central coast (Chap. 7, F). A few crosshatched sherds also occur intrusively in the El Palito (Barrancoid) sites of the Puerto Cabello area (Fig. 17). Finally, zoned crosshatching is characteristic of the Mag-

dalena and Sinú valleys of northwestern Colombia; and its occurrence in the Momíl culture of the latter valley seems to be approximately contemporaneous with its occurrence in Venezuela (Reichel-Dolmatoff, 1957).

When we discussed this distribution in our technical monograph (Cruxent and Rouse, 1958–59, p. 37), we were inclined to reject the possibility of a connection between

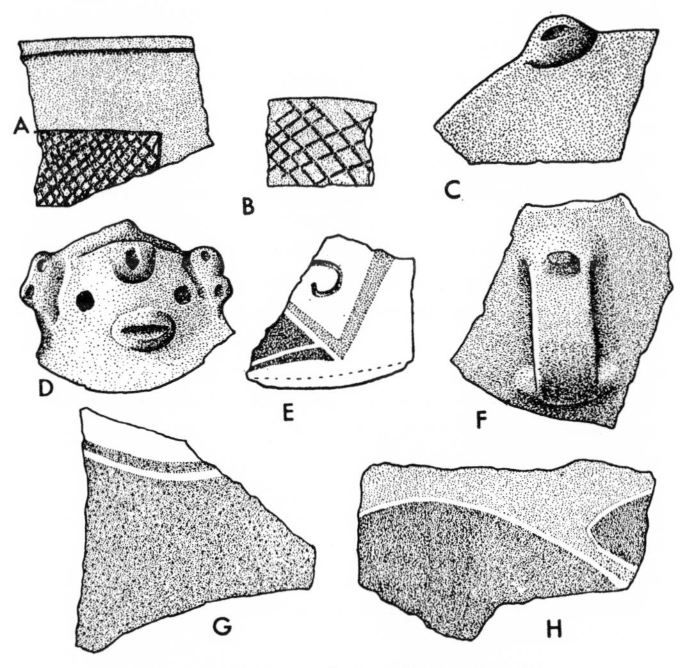

Fig. 30. Pottery of the El Mayal style

the zoned crosshatching of Colombia and that of Venezuela because there was such a difference in the designs of the two areas and so great a distance between them. But the gap has since been partially closed by the discovery of a few crosshatched sherds at the top of the Meso-Indian midden of Cerro Iguanas in the Tucacas area (Chap. 4, C) and by notice that there are a few such sherds in the collections made by de Josselin de Jong on the Dutch island of Aruba (Du Rhy and van Heekeren, 1960, pp. 88–89). In both cases, we may be dealing with trade sherds, as at El Palito. Nevertheless, the new occurrences do weaken the argument against deriving zoned crosshatching from Colombia.

2. The other possibility is that the Saladoid potters themselves developed zoned crosshatching, as well as the hollow-backed lugs, after they arrived on the coast but under stimulus of the Barrancoid series. It happens that the incised designs of the coastal styles, while made in the same technique as Barrancoid designs, are like the Saladoid painted designs in conception. From this, it may be inferred that the potters simply copied the painted designs in the technique of incision, possibly under Barrancoid stimulus. They did so by outlining with broad incised lines the areas ordinarily painted. They usually left these areas plain but sometimes filled them in with the fine crosshatching, which is reminiscent of the painted crosshatching they had done on the Orinoco (cf. Figs. 29 and 30). Hence, they may possibly have developed incised crosshatching as a substitute for paint, instead of acquiring it by diffusion from the west.

If this hypothesis is correct, the Río Guapo style must be regarded as an offshoot of the Saladoid series, resulting from diffusion to the west. The few crosshatched sherds found at El Palito, Cerro Iguanas, and on Aruba Island would then be trade sherds from the east, as is certainly true of a number of white-on-red painted sherds that were likewise found at El Palito (Chap. 7, A, F). And we would not need to postulate a connection with Colombia.

The Geochronometric Laboratory at Yale has just completed the analysis of a charcoal sample from the Río Guapo site that sheds light on this problem. Its date was A.D. 270 (Appendix, Y-1231), later than the earliest dates from the El Mayal and Irapa styles in the Carúpano and Güiria areas further east, which are A.D. 100 and 220 respectively; and so it indicates diffusion westward rather than eastward.

However, as we have said before (Chaps. 2, C; 6, B), it would be premature to draw a definite conclusion from a single radiocarbon date; our date, for example, may be from near the end of the period of existence of the Río Guapo style.

Alternative (2) has the advantages of being simpler and providing a better explanation of the stylistic relationships that have been discussed. And the technique of zoned crosshatching does seem to have been independently invented in the Amazon basin (Meggers and Evans, 1961); it could also have been independently invented in Venezuela.

For some reason, the zoned crosshatching and hollow-backed lugs did not survive very long in the Saladoid styles. Everywhere they are limited to the latter half of Period II and to the very beginning of Period III. They provide a good time marker for the latter half of Period II, combined as they are with great fineness of sherds and, in the Period II sites, an absence of flanges.

We tentatively conclude, then, that the Saladoid potters who moved from the Orinoco up to the coast developed certain traits which were lacking back on the Orinoco. The Saladoid people who continued out into the West Indies carried these traits with them, for the earliest pottery all the way out to Puerto Rico is characterized not only by the ubiquitous white-on-red painting and other Orinocan features of the Saladoid series but also by zoned crosshatching and hollow-backed lugs. As on the mainland, the latter traits survived only a short time, and therefore they provide a good horizon marker for the movement out as far as Puerto Rico.

A project to check the date of this movement by means of radiocarbon analysis is now under way. It has yielded the dates in Table 2, all of which are for pottery with the above-mentioned traits (Rouse, Alegría, and Stuiver, MS). Samples Y-1137 and Y-1138 came from the bottom layer at Morel, and Y-1136, from the middle layer, where the early Saladoid pottery terminates. (The top layer has yielded a subsequent style.) Similarly, sample Y-1233 came from the bottom of the Loiza site and Y-1232 from the top. Hence, these samples date the beginning and the end of the period of Saladoid expansion out to Puerto Rico at ca. A.D. 50 and 350, respectively.

The uniformity of the Saladoid pottery in the Lesser Antilles and Puerto Rico was broken after A.D. 400 by the development of a series of local styles. At the same time, there was further expansion into the rest of the Greater Antilles, again at the expense of the previous Meso-Indian inhabitants, who were eventually pushed back into the peripheral regions on the southwestern peninsula of Haiti and in the western and southern parts of Cuba where the first Spaniards encountered them (Rouse, 1951). This, however, takes us beyond the scope of the present book.

TABLE 2. DATES FOR THE SALADOID SPREAD INTO THE ANTILLES

Sample No.	*Island*	*Site*	*Style*	*Date before Present*	*Christian Date* (A.D.)
Y-1116	Martinique	La Salle	Undefined	1770 ± 80	130
Y-1136	Guadeloupe	Morel	Undefined	1380 ± 100	530
Y-1137	Guadeloupe	Morel	Undefined	1726 ± 70	170
Y-1138	Guadeloupe	Morel	Undefined	1705 ± 100	190
Y-1232	Puerto Rico	Loiza	Hacienda Grande	1580 ± 80	370
Y-1233	Puerto Rico	Loiza	Hacienda Grande	1830 ± 80	120

That the Neo-Indians migrated from Venezuela into the West Indies, pushing back the Meso-Indians as they went, has been known for some time. Our researches shed new light on the background of this migration in Venezuela, showing that it formed part of the movement of Saladoid people out of the lower Orinoco valley as the result of dispossession by the Barrancoid people. The Saladoid refugees migrated first to the Peninsula of Paria and there they split, part of them turning west to the Venezuelan coast and islands and the rest continuing north into the Antilles. Both groups encountered Meso-Indians, who had survived longer en masse in northeastern Venezuela and in the Antilles than in other parts of the Caribbean area, presumably because those two regions were the most isolated; and both groups pushed these Meso-Indians back into peripheral regions, e.g., into the delta of the Orinoco River and to the remote parts of Haiti and Cuba.

Returning to the nature of Saladoid pottery, let us dis-

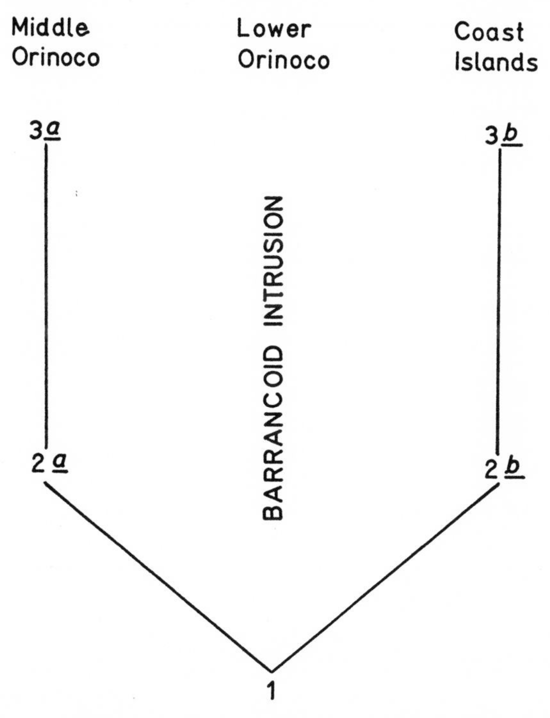

Fig. 31. Stages in the development of the Saladoid series

cuss the trends within the series more directly. It passed through three stages of development, the second and third of which may be divided into two parts, one above the Barrancoid intrusion, in the middle and upper Orinoco valley, and the other below the intrusion, on the eastern coast and islands. Stage (1) consists of the Saladero style and possibly the earliest pottery at Ronquín; (2a) is the intermediate pottery at Ronquín; (2b), the Irapa and El Mayal styles; (3a), the Cotua style and possibly the latest pottery of the Ronquín style; and (3b), the Chuare and El Agua styles (Fig. 28). The relationships among these groups are diagrammed in Figure 31. The trends may be summarized as follows:

1. The pottery of group (1) is thin and fine; of (2a) and (3b), less so; and of (3a) and (3b), relatively thick and coarse.

2. Rims are only plain or beveled in (1), while flanges are added in the latter part of (2b) and in (3a) and (3b). Stages (2a), (2b), and (3a) also developed a distinctive type of rectangularly ridged rim.

3. The knobbed lugs of (1) were simple and geometric. In (2a) and (3a) these developed, apparently under Barrancoid influence, into human and animal heads, rounded in shape and supplied with modeled-incised features. Somewhat similar lugs made their appearance in (2b) and (3b) but they are more variable. In (2b) they include a distinctive hollow-backed form.

4. Stage (1) had only simple, typically Saladoid incision. This persisted and became more elaborate, presumably under Barrancoid influence, in (2a) and (3a). The incision of (2b) and (3b) developed in a different direction, though supposedly under the same Barrancoid influence, by imitating the white-on-red painted designs. Stage (2b) also has zoned crosshatching, which we have interpreted as a substitute for zoned painting.

5. Typically Barrancoid incised designs were used to decorate the flanges added in (3a) and (3b).

6. Red designs on a plain background became extinct at the end of stage (1).

Despite these changes, there are a number of traits which persisted throughout all stages and in both branches of the series, as follows:

1. The open bowl with flat base and flaring sides.
2. Tapered and beveled rims.

3. Vertical strap handles, frequently surmounted by lugs.
4. Flat, tabular lugs attached to the rim.
5. The use of red paint to cover limited areas of the vessel surface.
6. White-on-red painted designs, consisting typically of zones bordered by thin lines.

In these persistences and changes we may see the gradual differentiation and divergence of two groups of styles within the Saladoid series. If group (3a) had not died out in the face of Arauquinoid expansion at the end of Period III, it might have continued to lose or to modify the typical Saladoid traits to such an extent that it would have become a new and entirely distinct series. This did happen on the coast with the rise of the Guayabitoid series out of (3b), and in the Greater Antilles, where Cuevas, the final Saladoid style, gave rise to Ostiones, which ultimately developed into a new series, the Chicoid (Cruxent and Rouse, 1958–59, Fig. 4).

Saladoid pottery comes only from the refuse of habitation, which contains many fish bones and, on the coast, shells. These indicate that food from the river and sea formed an important part of the people's diet. Fragments of griddles are common in all the sites, testifying to the importance of manioc in the diet. There are surprisingly few artifacts of other kinds. At Saladero, for example, we found only cylindrical pot rests of clay, flint chips, cylindrical stone beads, and a bone awl. Ceremonial objects are lacking.

B. GUAYABITOID SERIES

Guayabitoid, the successor to the Saladoid series on the east coast, remains to be discussed. It consists of two Venezuelan styles, Guayabita itself around Güiria on the Peninsula of Paria and El Morro in the Carúpano area further west (Fig. 32). The Bontour style of Trinidad also belongs to this series (Rouse, 1953b, pp. 97–98).

Osgood and Howard (1943) trenched the Guayabita site

in 1941, and we dug three other sites of the style in 1961. We tested three sites of the El Morro style in 1955, in one of which El Morro refuse overlay that of the Chuare style, a Period III member of the Saladoid series. This leads us to place the Guayabitoid series in Period IV, a placement which is confirmed by radiocarbon dates of A.D. 1240 for the Guayabita style and A.D. 1210 for El Morro. A second

EPOCHS	PERIODS	COAST: Carúpano Area	COAST: Güiria Area	PERIODS	DATES
Indo-Hispanic	V	EL MORRO		V	1500 A.D.
Neo-Indian	IV		GUAYABITA	IV	1000 A.D.
	III			III	300 A.D.
	II			II	1000 B.C.
Meso-Indian	I			I	5000 B.C.
Paleo-Indian					15,000

Fig. 32. Chronology of the Guayabitoid series

date of A.D. 1650 for El Morro indicates that it, at least, survived into Period V (Appendix, Y-1111, Y-298, Y-299).

Both styles are simple, comprising ollas with flat or annular bases (Fig. 33, C), plain rims, and simple wedge-shaped tabs or cylindrical lugs (Fig. 33, A). Guayabita pottery also has crude incised and appliqué designs (Fig. 33, B). The Bontour style, prevalent in Trinidad during Period IV, is quite similar.

Irapa, the preceding Saladoid style of the Paria Peninsula, shows a transition into Guayabita by a process of simplification, its later sites having less and less decoration. Hence, we assume that the series originated on the Peninsula of Paria and spread from there eastward to Trinidad, in the form of the Bontour style, and westward to the Carúpano area, in the form of the El Morro style. These spreads may

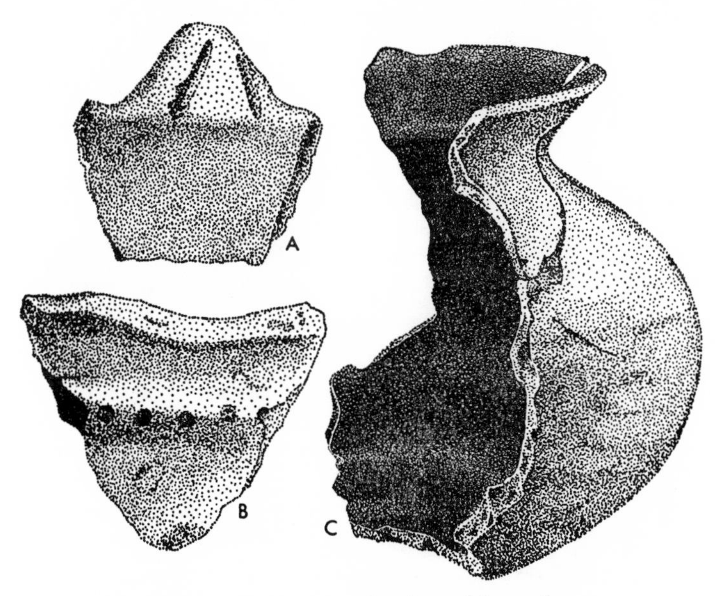

Fig. 33. Pottery of the Guayabita style

have been by migration, since no transitional form is known on Trinidad or in the Carúpano area.

C. CABRANTICA STYLE

During our 1961 excavations on the Peninsula of Paria, we discovered a new style of pottery at the site of Cabrantica, east of Güiria (see Fig. 2). Its refuse overlay that of the Irapa style, from which we obtained a radiocarbon date of A.D. 570 (Appendix, Y-1112); it is cross-dated by trade sherds with the Los Barrancos and Guayabita styles, there being sherds of both these styles in the Cabrantica site and Cabrantica sherds in the Guayabita site. Therefore, we place

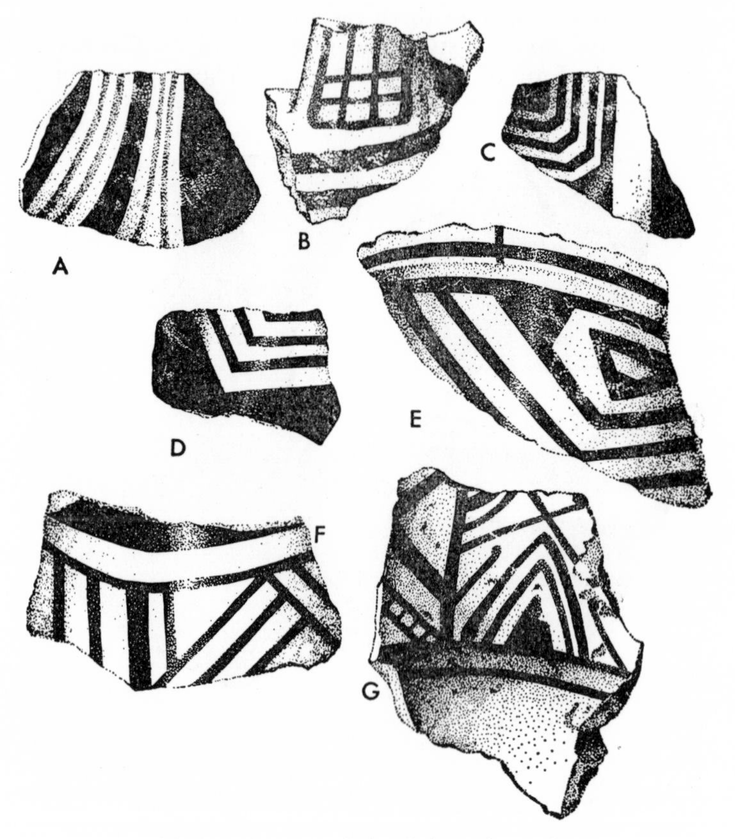

Fig. 34. Pottery of the Cabrantica style

the Cabrantica style in the latter part of Period III and in Period IV (Fig. 3).

The sherds are heavily tempered with quartz particles. They come from bowls and ollas with flat bases and an occasional hollow rim. There are both vertical and horizontal handles of the rod and strap types and simple lugs, mainly of tabular shape and geometric design. Incision and appliqué work both yield to painting as the principal form of decoration. Designs are rectilinear and are done in red and/or black on a white background (Fig. 34).

The Cabrantica painting attracts attention because it is of the western type; it would be at home in either the Ocumaroid or the Dabajuroid series. How this form of painting reached the Peninsula of Paria remains to be determined. Its closest occurrence is in the Punta Arenas style of the Cumaná area, which is a member of the Dabajuroid series, but Punta Arenas has many traits which are lacking in Cabrantica, such as rim corrugations, hollow legs, and curvilinear designs. In the absence of these traits, Cabrantica cannot be placed in the Dabajuroid series. Nevertheless, it must be regarded as the easternmost penetration of the western form of painting.

Chapter 9

INDO-HISPANIC EPOCH

Christopher Columbus, embarking in 1498 upon his third voyage, turned toward South America and on June 30 discovered an island which he called Trinidad. He saw land farther west and, believing it to be an island, named it Isla de Gracia, although it was actually the Peninsula of Paria. He then explored the Gulf of Paria, passed through the Dragon's Mouth between Trinidad and Paria, and was carried westward along the Caribbean coast by the prevailing winds and currents. Natives told him that there were pearl fisheries in the vicinity but, despite the importance of this news to Spain, which was hungering for new sources of wealth, he did not tarry to investigate it, for his eyes bothered him and he was anxious to reach Santo Domingo. On August 15, he came within sight of Margarita Island, which he called Asunción, and then proceeded northward across the Caribbean Sea (Morison, 1942, vol. 2, pp. 233–93).

It is to be supposed that the news of the pearl fisheries caused a sensation in Santo Domingo and eventually in Spain. Certainly it inspired a series of voyages by explorers greedy for pearls. For example, in the very next year, 1499, a group of pilots from Spain, including Alonso de Ojeda and Amerigo Vespucci, visited Paria and Margarita before continuing west along the coast of Venezuela (Gil Fortoul, 1942, pp. 20–21). There may have been even earlier voyages from Santo Domingo, though these are undocumented.

The voyagers soon discovered that the principal pearl fisheries were situated on Cubagua Island. We lack records of the first Spanish contacts with the Indians of that island but it is logical to assume that extensive trade for pearls arose almost immediately. As Guillermo Morón (1954, p. 69) has put it:

> . . . in addition to [the voyages] known and authorized, others may have been undertaken without official knowledge, out of sheer desire for profit or perhaps in the nature of espionage; but in any case there were voyages which are not known today for lack of documentation. . . . And these voyages unknown to history were made not only by Spaniards but also by people of other nationalities, such as the Englishmen encountered by Ojeda during his first voyage.

Our studies of Indo-Hispanic archaeology support Morón's conclusion; we have established it as a fact that potsherds of European manufacture occur among the indigenous artifacts on Cubagua Island.

The original European settlers of Venezuela came to Cubagua Island from Santo Domingo shortly after the beginning of the sixteenth century. They, too, were attracted by the pearl fisheries and they built a town from which to operate them. This town, Nueva Cadiz, was the first in South America, the mainland being still inhabited only by Indians. It flourished for several decades, during which time the Spaniards brought Indians from all parts of the continent, as well as Negroes from Africa, to work as slaves in its pearl fisheries. It grew in size and the wealthier people constructed permanent buildings of masonry. Eventually, however, the fisheries became exhausted, and Nueva Cadiz was abandoned about the middle of the century.

Meanwhile, Trinidad, Margarita, and Cumaná on the mainland were being more or less successfully colonized from Cubagua. In the west, the present Dutch islands of

Curaçao and Bonaire similarly served as bases from which towns such as Coro, Maracaibo, and El Tocuyo were established on the mainland. Not all of the new towns contained masonry buildings, as had Nueva Cadiz. The less wealthy settlements, such as San Cristobal de los Cumanagotos at Maurica, near the present city of Barcelona, had only thatched huts of the native type.

From the towns mentioned, expeditions set out to explore the rest of Venezuela, with the result that there was widespread contact between Europeans and Indians during the latter part of the sixteenth century. Our archaeological sites yield evidence of this contact in the form of European trade objects, especially European pottery and majolica, which provide us with the means of dating the sites and the styles of native pottery that coexisted in the sites with Spanish pottery.

The European population continued to expand. The Valencia basin was settled in 1547, Caracas in 1567, and the present city of Barcelona was founded in 1637. As the land was settled, its Indians were rounded up, assigned to farms known as *encomiendas,* and forced to work there for the settlers as virtual slaves. The system of *encomiendas* was abolished during the latter part of the sixteenth century, and thereafter the Indians were free to come and go as they pleased. In the vicinity of Spanish settlements, they gradually became assimilated, contributing to the process of transculturation whereby Western, African, and Indian cultures have all contributed to the development of modern American civilization.

The first settlers were accompanied by priests who labored to convert the Indians, but it was not until the middle of the seventeenth century that a systematic organization of missions came into existence. Missions were especially numerous in the Llanos, where they functioned as cattle ranches. The missionaries regularly visited the surviving tribes of Indians to obtain recruits for these missions. Once there, the Indians lived by themselves and raised their own food, but they had to contribute labor to the missions and were subject to its rules, which minutely regulated their lives, with the result that they gradually lost their native cultures.

The missions declined during the eighteenth century and the wars of independence finally put an end to them. Since then, the only unassimilated Indians have been those who live away from the European settlements, especially in the delta of the Orinoco, Venezuelan Guiana, Amazonas, and along the Colombian frontier, where many tribes preserve their native cultures.

Certain items of aboriginal culture have survived as folk customs in various parts of Venezuela. Among the most interesting of these is pottery. The quality of the Indian pottery was such that European methods of manufacture—e.g., the use of the wheel—have been slow to spread to the countryside, and today we still find survivals of the aboriginal methods of making pottery even among Venezuelans of European extraction, e.g., at Manicuare near Cumaná (Gines, Cayetano de Carrocera, Cruxent, and Rísquez, 1946, pp. 185–86).

From this brief review of the history of Indo-Hispanic contacts, it will be apparent that there should be several different kinds of sites dating from the Indo-Hispanic epoch: ruins of the first Spanish towns, containing the artifacts of Indian *encomenderos;* remains of Indian settlements, including European trade objects; and mission sites. There are, of course, also the remains of purely European settlements, but these do not concern us here.

The purely Indian sites, with objects obtained from Europeans by trade, need not be discussed either, since they do not differ significantly from the remains of the Neo-Indian epoch which have already been described. No mission sites have as yet been excavated, though we have surface collections from several of them. We are left, therefore, only with the Spanish-Indian settlements, two of which will serve to illustrate the archaeology of the epoch—Nueva Cadiz and Maurica.

A. NUEVA CADIZ

As has already been noted, Nueva Cadiz was the first Spanish town in South America. It is situated on Cubagua Island, where it succeeded the long series of Meso- and Neo-Indian settlements we have been discussing. The Neo-Indians were accustomed to fish for pearls, and these attracted the Spaniards soon after the beginning of the sixteenth century, as we have seen.

The site passed through three phases. The Spaniards first came there from Santo Domingo in order to trade for pearls. They did not establish permanent settlements but camped on the island three to four months a year while trading.

Gradually, the Spaniards began to enslave the Indians and to take over control of the pearl fisheries. It was in this phase that they settled down, building simple huts of clay and straw. They had to abandon the settlement in 1520, however, because of a rebellion by the Indians of Cumaná on the adjacent mainland. The Cubagua settlers feared an attack by these Indians; and in addition they were dependent upon the mainland for drinking water and other supplies (Simon Velásquez, 1956, p. 50).

Construction of a fortress at Cumaná in 1523 brought the Indians under control and ushered in the third and most productive phase in the occupation of Cubagua Island. More permanent buildings of stone were constructed and in 1528 the town officially received the name of Nueva Cadiz. It reached the peak of its development between 1530 and 1535, when it may have had a population of 1,500. Thereafter, it declined rapidly, as the pearl fisheries became exhausted. Hurricanes and attacks by pirates probably hastened the end, and by 1550 the site had been abandoned (Otte, 1961, pp. xxiv–liv).

At its height, Nueva Cadiz contained not only Spaniards and a few Negro slaves but also a large number of Indian slaves who had been brought from all over the Caribbean to work in the pearl fisheries. Great quantities of pearls were obtained, and wealth accumulated in the town. It became an important commercial center, trading not only with other Spanish settlements but also with the Indians of the mainland. Eventually, it obtained political control over Cumaná and over the larger island of Margarita. But these were secondary functions; when the pearl fisheries declined, Nueva Cadiz was unable to survive because it could not obtain enough food and water from such an arid environment.

In December 1954 John M. Goggin, of the University of Florida, and Cruxent visited Nueva Cadiz in order to collect Spanish pottery for comparison with material they had excavated at other contemporary sites. They dug in the floor of a house and were fortunate enough to discover a pot full of pearls, which had apparently been stored there by a Spanish settler. The pearls had deteriorated to the point where they no longer had any commercial value, but the find aroused great popular interest and Cruxent was able to obtain funds from the Venezuelan government with which to make extensive excavations. The work was carried out continuously from 1955 through 1961, and a large part of the ruins has been uncovered and stabilized (Pl. 48, A). It is planned to build a small museum at the site and to develop it as a tourist attraction (Cruxent, 1955; Cruxent and Rolando, 1961).

At the start of excavation, the site consisted of a series of low mounds of earth, separated from the shore by enormous piles of shells, a by-product of the pearl fisheries. Excavation revealed no traces of masonry construction in the lower part of the refuse, which was apparently deposited during the first two phases of occupation noted above. Remnants of masonry walls, constructed during the third phase of occupation, lay close to the surface. They are limited to the windward side of the site, extending along two sides of a point in the shape of an L. Behind them and away from the shore, even the uppermost refuse lacks walls. It is believed that this part of the site was inhabited by the Indian and Negro slaves, who would have lived in less permanent dwellings. Burials are scattered throughout the site (Pl. 49).

In the Spanish section of the town the walls were built of uncut stones, taken from the interior of the island (Pl. 48, B). These were chinked with clay and plastered with lime, made by grinding up coral. Clay bricks were also used occasionally. The floors were of earth and the flat roofs were made of reeds plastered with clay.

The buildings were arranged in regular, rectangular blocks. The largest and most elaborate houses lie along the southeast side of the point, where the trade winds have the greatest cooling effect. There is also a church in this area. A monastery lies on a side street, toward the center of the site, and another church, called "the hermitage," is off by itself at the leeward end of the L.

The monastery is the largest and most interesting structure. Its front part consists of a great rectangular room, which probably served as a church. There are several graves at the end of this room, one of which is covered with bricks and has a groove around its edge, where an iron grating may once have stood. Doors lead from this room into a number of others. One may have been the base of a church tower, others are supposed to have served as living quarters, and a larger one is identified as a kitchen. The building contains two patios, one of them quite large.

The greater part of the stone sculpture found at Nueva Cadiz has come from the monastery. It includes several elaborately carved gargoyles (Pls. 54, A; 55, A), a column (Pl. 54, B), and shields (Pls. 54, C; 55, B). One of the last bears the Franciscan coat of arms, a fact which has led to identification of the structure as the monastery of San Francisco (Cruxent, 1955, p. 4). Stone for the carvings was not available locally and is believed to have been brought from the Peninsula of Araya, on the nearby mainland, and carved on the spot, though some observers have claimed that the sculptures were imported from Europe.

The houses come directly up to the street and are entered by a door in front. A typical house consists of four rooms: a living room and a bedroom in front, and a storeroom and kitchen behind them. There is a walled patio in back, considerably smaller than that of the monastery. In the patios may have lived Indian slaves who acted as household servants for the monks and the burghers.

Some houses have masonry stairways which must have led to second stories; one of them turns a corner. There are also smaller rooms in the walls which may have served as closets. The doors swung on round sockets and fitted into recesses in the jambs, presumably in order to keep out the cold wind at night. Kitchens have a rectangular hearth of masonry, raised about 50 cm. above the floor.

To the west of the houses, Cruxent found a series of borrow pits, from which clay had been obtained for constructing the buildings. These were filled with refuse. One is lined with stones and may have served as an underground storage chamber. Several nearby holes, of smaller size, can be identified as wells. There was also a circular area of burnt stone which may have been a lime kiln.

The refuse yielded considerable numbers of animal bones. A study of these by Wing (1961) has revealed that the inhabitants relied most heavily upon seafood, including turtles and fish (e.g., the porgy, catfish, and ray). Wild animals, such as the deer and rabbit, ranked next and then birds (the pelican, booby, cormorant, muscovy duck, and black vulture). Domesticated animals were the least frequent, which is not surprising since the aridity of the climate would have made it difficult to raise them. Only pigs and chickens were at all common.

Potsherds of Spanish manufacture abounded in the refuse. These include majolica (Pl. 50, B), various kinds of glazed ware (Pls. 50, A; 52, A), olive jars (Pls. 51; 52, B, C), and Chinese porcelain. There are also stamps (Pl. 53), tiles, and downspouts of clay. Glass was used for goblets and beads, which were traded to the Indians; iron, for knives and other implements; and copper, for a variety of ornaments, as well as for needles and thimbles.

The Indian pottery falls into two groups. First, there is the pottery of foreign styles, which the Indians must have brought with them from various parts of the Caribbean as they were enslaved. This includes some as yet unidentified material from the Greater Antilles and examples of all the late Neo-Indian series of Venezuela: Arauquinoid, Dabajuroid, Memoid, Tierroid, and Valencioid.

Second, there is a new style which the Indians apparently developed after they arrived on Nueva Cadiz and which we have named after the site. The potsherds are crude, heavily tempered with crushed rock and shell, limited in shape to simple bowls and jars, and decorated only with a few rod handles and rectilinear designs in red, white, yellow, and black. This Nueva Cadiz style marks the beginning of a process of simplification which is evident in all late historic Indian styles of eastern Venezuela—e.g., Tras de la Vela on the Peninsula of Araya—and which has culminated in the modern folk pottery of Manicuare on the same peninsula (Cruxent and Rouse, 1958–59, p. 116).

B. MAURICA

To discuss Maurica after Nueva Cadiz is anticlimactic, since its culture is so much less highly developed. Nevertheless, it will serve to illustrate a later period of time and a more normal form of Spanish-Indian contact, unaffected by the pearl fisheries or, indeed, by the custom of slavery, since this had been abolished by the time Maurica was founded at the end of the sixteenth century.

Maurica is situated just outside the city of Barcelona and west of the mouth of the Río Neverí (see Fig. 2). It consists of a series of small shell middens, ranging up to a meter in height. The authors discovered this site in 1955 and dug a test pit there. Cruxent subsequently made a second and larger excavation.

The only traces of construction at Maurica are a few fragments of brick. Yet Spanish artifacts are as abundant as at Nueva Cadiz, including pottery, glassware, and various kinds of metal artifacts. Ferrous slag is common, indicating that iron was worked at the site; and we encountered many bones of domesticated animals. Indian pottery is also very common; it resembles the Nueva Cadiz style in most respects but has preserved a few local traits, such as fabric impression and corrugation of the neck.

Maurica is also known as Sabana de los Cumanagotos, and local tradition has it that the site was occupied during early colonial time by the Cumanagoto Indians. However, the Spanish artifacts obtained by us are of a later date, and the site may better be identified as San Cristobal de los Cumanagotos, which was inhabited toward the end of the sixteenth and the beginning of the seventeenth centuries by a mixed group of Spaniards and Indians (personal communication from Sr. Salomón de Lima). The site illustrates the process of fusion between the two which eventually led to integration of the Indians within the Spanish population throughout the civilized parts of Venezuela.

Chapter 10

SUMMARY AND CONCLUSIONS

Two approaches to Venezuelan archaeology have been combined in this study. One is chronological: we have been able to distinguish a succession of four epochs and have assigned the remains to these epochs by means of stratigraphy, radiocarbon analyses, and other techniques. The second may be termed ethnic: we have identified a large number of local complexes or styles and, insofar as possible, have assembled these into twelve series, each of which represents a discrete group of people having distinctive cultural traits. In summarizing the epochs and series, we shall emphasize and expand upon the principal cultural achievements of each.

Paleo-Indian epoch. The Paleo-Indians are supposed to have entered the New World from Siberia by way of Alaska and central Canada, and to have continued southward through the United States and Middle America into South America. We have estimated that they arrived in Venezuela about 15,000 B.C., primarily upon the basis of evidence from the site of Muaco, near the city of Coro on the western coast. Muaco consists of a spring, to which the mammals of the vicinity came to drink. Man waylaid the animals there and killed and ate them, as is evidenced by the presence of cut and burned bones and of Paleo-Indian implements in the muck surrounding the spring (Pl. 4). Two of the burned bones have yielded radiocarbon dates of 14,920 and 12,780 B.C. respectively. Many of the bones came from animals now extinct, such as the mastodon, giant sloth, and New World horse; this is in itself evidence of great antiquity.

The site of Muaco may be attributed to our earliest known series, Joboid, but it does not tell us much about the nature of this series since the Indians did not actually live there. We have defined the series in terms of Cruxent's finds in the region of El Jobo, inland from Muaco. Here, the Joboid people lived on a series of successive terraces formed by the Río Pedregal. The earliest people, who occupied the uppermost terraces, made only crude choppers and scrapers of quartzite, which might have been used to manufacture wooden spears. To these were added a succession of new types on the lower, and therefore later, terraces: first, bifacially worked blades, which may have been hafted in thrusting spears or used as axes or knives; then, lanceolate projectile points, presumably for throwing spears; and finally a few stemmed projectile points (Pl. 3). It is assumed that the spears were used to hunt mammals of the kinds found at Muaco, although no bones were recovered in the sites. It would be surprising if the Joboid Indians did not also hunt smaller game and gather wild vegetable foods, although evidence of these, too, is lacking.

Meso-Indian epoch. By 5000 B.C., when the Meso-Indian epoch began, the big game animals upon which the Paleo-Indians had relied for much of their food had become extinct. Nevertheless, some of the Meso-Indians continued to emphasize hunting, as evidenced by the widespread occurrence of stone projectile points throughout Venezuelan Guayana, especially at the camp site of Canaima (Pl. 6). These points are of the same stemmed type which first appeared on the latest terraces of the El Jobo region, and therefore they may be regarded as a survival of the Joboid tradition of stoneworking into the Meso-Indian epoch.

Elsewhere, the Meso-Indians ceased to manufacture stone

points, and came to rely upon new sources of food. Along the coast, they turned to fishing and shell fishing, and in so doing developed maritime skills which enabled them to colonize the nearby islands for the first time. Both on the mainland and on the islands their places of habitation are marked by large piles of shells which bear witness to their dependence upon seafood.

Several different series are probably represented among these shell heaps, but so far we have been able to recognize only one, which we have named Manicuaroid. It is best known from our excavations at Punta Gorda, on Cubagua Island off Cumaná in eastern Venezuela. Habitation began there about 2325 B.C., according to a radiocarbon date from the bottom of the site, and continued until after the time of Christ, as indicated by the appearance of trade pottery at the top of the site. Additional sites of the Manicuaroid series have been found along the adjacent mainland and on Margarita Island; and the Manicuaroid people may also have played a part in the colonization of the West Indies, although this is a disputed point.

The Manicuaroid Indians used bone projectile points instead of the stone points of the Joboid Indians. They made small, bipointed stones, possibly for use in slings, and shell implements, which increased in variety and complexity as the series developed. Gouges fashioned from the outer whorl of the conch shell (Pl. 7, A) made their appearance midway in the series; these may well have been used to hollow dugout canoes, with which to travel from the coast to the islands. Shell pendants, shaped somewhat like incisor teeth, and a crude petroglyph are also noteworthy (Pls. 7, C; 8, C). Burial was directly in the refuse without grave objects.

A different kind of development seems to have taken place in the interior of Venezuela during the Meso-Indian epoch. We are only beginning to obtain evidence of this development at the site of Rancho Peludo in the Maracaibo basin, not far from the Colombian border, and we have had to fill out the data from this site with knowledge from similar sites in other parts of the world. Since Rancho

Peludo is in the interior, its inhabitants were unable to turn to maritime foods as the Pleistocene game became extinct. Instead, they probably began to rely upon fruits and wild vegetable foods. From these, it would have been only a short step to the cultivation of fruits and vegetables, i.e., to the beginnings of agriculture. It is unlikely, however, that the first agriculture was very effective; the crops and the techniques for producing them were undoubtedly too rudimentary to do more than supplement the gathering of wild fruits and vegetables.

Agriculture is indicated at Rancho Peludo by the presence of clay griddles similar to the *budares* still used in many parts of Venezuela to bake bread made from manioc roots. Pottery vessels also occur for the first time; they include simple bowls or jars with plain or annular bases, fabric-marked surfaces, and crude appliqué decoration (Pl. 9). The pottery was used both as utensils and for burial urns, which are surprisingly elaborate for this early period, between 2820 and 445 B.C., according to our radiocarbon dates.

Neo-Indian epoch. The start of the Neo-Indian epoch is put at the time when agriculture had developed sufficiently to replace hunting, fishing, and gathering as the principal means of subsistence. This happened about 1000 B.C. in eastern Venezuela but may have been later in the west, to judge by our radiocarbon dates from Rancho Peludo. In eastern Venezuela, manioc remained the basic crop, but in the west the Neo-Indians seem to have preferred corn, which had been domesticated in Middle America, according to current theory, and had spread south and east from there via Colombia.

The Meso-Indian way of life survived for awhile in certain areas, especially on the east coast and adjacent islands. Indeed, a few groups of people, such as the Warrau Indians of the Orinoco delta, continued as Meso-Indians into the Indo-Hispanic epoch, but most turned to the new form of life, adopting not only agriculture but also pottery, unless, as at Rancho Peludo, they already had them.

The new emphasis upon agriculture did not cause the

Neo-Indians to abandon their previous means of subsistence. Their coastal sites are full of shells, indicating continued consumption of seafood. But agriculture apparently did enable the Indians to develop larger communities—villages rather than camps—and more elaborate forms of social and political organization, art, and religion. Too few traces of these have survived for them to be used as the basis for isolating groups of Neo-Indians. Instead, we have had to rely upon pottery, which is the only common kind of artifact in the Neo-Indian sites. We have been able to distinguish a large number of local styles and to assemble them into ten series, each of which is indicative of a separate group of Neo-Indians, as follows:

1. The Dabajuroid series appears to have had its origin in the pottery of Rancho Peludo, already described in connection with the Meso-Indian epoch. It continued in the same region, i.e., within the Maracaibo basin, throughout the Neo-Indian epoch and, beginning about A.D. 1000, also spread southward into the Venezuelan Andes, northward to the present Dutch islands of Aruba and Curaçao, and eastward along the coast as far as Cumaná in eastern Venezuela (Fig. 9). It is characterized by perforated annular bases, fabric impression on the lower part of the body, corrugation of the neck, appliqué work, and, in the later styles, by bulging hollow legs and complex designs painted in black and/or red on a white background (Pl. 12). These latter traits may well have been obtained from the Tocuyanoid series (2). Urn burial continues from the previous period, and the presence of figurines attests to a certain religious development.
2. The Tocuyanoid series centers around Quibor, near Barquisimeto at the base of the Venezuelan Andes, where we obtained a radiocarbon date of 295 B.C. From there, it apparently spread southeastward into the Llanos and northeastward to and along the coast as far as Maiquetía, the airport for Caracas (Fig. 11). Between A.D. 300 and 1000 it gave way to a pair of related series, Tierroid (3) and Ocumaroid (4). From its very beginning it had hol-

low bulbous legs; elaborate curvilinear designs which were either incised or painted in red and black on a white background; and simple modeling and painting of snakes and human faces (Pls. 13–16). Many of these traits are also to be found on the pottery of northeastern Colombia and Central America, and we believe that they originally diffused into Venezuela from that direction. Too little is yet known about the series to discuss its nonceramic aspects.

3. The Tierroid series, like Tocuyanoid, centers in the region around Barquisimeto, extending down from there onto the western Llanos and up into the Andes of Trujillo and Mérida (Fig. 13). It dates from A.D. 1000 to 1500. Its pottery continues the Tocuyanoid emphasis upon hollow bulbous legs and polychrome painting but lacks its incision and modeling (Pls. 17–19). The Tierroid people were responsible for the most elaborate kinds of archaeological monuments in Venezuela, the causeways of earth on the Llanos and the shaft graves and shrine caves in the Andes; and they (or their neighbors) produced the greatest variety of ceremonial objects, including incense burners, amulets, and figurines of various types (Pls. 26–29).

4. The Ocumaroid series succeeds Tocuyanoid in the coastal part of the latter's distribution, i.e., in the region from Tucacas to La Guaira. It began about A.D. 500 and some of its styles survived until the arrival of Europeans (Fig. 23). It combines the Tocuyanoid form of painting with features of two other series which impinged upon that part of the coast, Dabajuroid (1) and Barrancoid (5), e.g., it has corrugation and appliqué work which are reminiscent of the former series and some modeling-incision from the latter (Fig. 24). Despite this richness of ceramics, the Ocumaroid people did not produce monuments of any kind; they have left only deposits of refuse. No sure traces of ceremonial activity have yet been found in the refuse, but they are not necessarily lacking, for relatively little excavation has been done.

5. The Barrancoid series is in two parts rather distant

from each other, one in the Valencia basin and on the adjacent coast and the other around the delta of the Orinoco River (Fig. 17). Our earliest radiocarbon date for the central Venezuelan part of the series is A.D. 260 and for the Orinocan part, 985 B.C. They are characterized by solid annular bases, flanges attached to the rim and incised with curvilinear designs, and elaborate modeled-incised figures on the vessel wall or on lugs attached to the rim (Pls. 31–35). Clay pipes bearing similar decoration occur in association with the central part of the series; presumably, these had a religious significance, as among the North American Indians. Archaeologists have been attracted to the Barrancoid series by the distinctiveness and complexity of its decoration and have proposed various theories to account for its origin, but these remain speculative. We do not even know how the two segments of the series were related; we can only theorize that both are derived from a third as yet undiscovered segment on the Llanos de Apure, whence the series may have spread northward via the Rios Portuguesa and Pao into the Valencia basin and onto the coast, and eastward down the Orinoco River to the Barrancas region, to Trinidad, and to northwestern British Guiana.

6. If there actually was a segment of the Barrancoid series on the Llanos de Apure, it could have been ancestral to the Arauquinoid series, which arose there during the latter part of the first millennium A.D. and subsequently spread down the Orinoco River, putting an end to the Orinocan segment of the Barrancoid tradition about A.D. 1000 (Fig. 19). The Arauquinoid series retains certain Barrancoid traits, such as modeled-incised lugs, but is distinguished by the used of sponge spicules as a tempering material, by bowls surmounted with collars or small lugs decorated with appliqué features, and by beveled rims bearing incised and excised designs. Incision and excision were also used in the production of cylindrical stamps of clay (Pl. 38, B). The Arauquinoid people built mounds of earth in order to raise their houses above

the floods which inundated the Llanos during rainy seasons, and some of them also produced figurines.

7. The Valencioid series, as its name implies, centers in the Valencia basin, extending eastward through the mountains as far as Caracas, down to the coast in the La Guaira and Río Chico areas, and out on to the Los Roques Islands, off La Guaira. It dates between A.D. 1000 and 1600 (Fig. 21). The excavations of Requena (1932), Bennett (1937), Osgood (1943), and Kidder (1944) in the mounds around Lake Valencia, have made it the best known of all Venezuelan pottery, though it is relatively simple. It consists of bowls with biomorphic lugs and collared jars bearing faces. The features of both are done in appliqué work, of which the coffee-bean eye is typical. There is no painting and little incision. Figurines, amulets, and urn burials have also been found in the Valencia mounds (Frontispiece; Pls. 39–46). The Valencioid series is presumably a degeneration from the Barrancoid series (5), with the addition of traits from the Arauquinoid series (6).

8. The Memoid series is known from the north central Llanos south of Caracas and from the coast around Río Chico. It was in existence during protohistoric and early historic times. Its simple globular vessels were typically roughened by one of a series of techniques: corrugation, incision, scoring, punctation, the addition of tiny lumps of clay, or the pressing of fingers or fabrics into the wet clay. The sites are likewise simple; nothing has so far been found in them except utilitarian artifacts.

9. The Saladoid series made its appearance in the middle and lower Orinoco valley by 1000 B.C. from an as yet undetermined source. Soon after 1000 B.C., the movement of Barrancoid people into the lower part of the Orinoco valley split the Saladoid people in two. One group remained in the middle part of the Orinoco valley (Howard, 1943) while the other moved out through the Orinoco delta to the northeast coast of Venezuela, Margarita, Trinidad, and on into the rest of the West Indies, over-

whelming the Meso-Indian inhabitants of those areas as it went (Fig. 28). The two groups persisted in Venezuela until about A.D. 1000, when the southern one became acculturated to the Araquinoid series (6) and the northern one was transformed into several local variants, including the Guayabitoid series (10) in northeastern Venezuela and the Chicoid series of the Greater Antilles. In its pure form, the Saladoid series was characterized by flat bases, bowls shaped like an inverted bell, vertical strap handles, and white-on-red painted designs. To these were added many Barrancoid traits after the Barrancoid Indians moved into the lower Orinoco valley (Figs. 29, 30). There is no trace of any ceremonial activity; even the burials are simple, and almost all lack grave objects.

10. The Guayabitoid series may be regarded as a degeneration from Saladoid, in which the olla became predominant, handles and painting died out, tabular lugs were simplified, and modeling-incision was replaced by crude incised and appliqué designs (Fig. 33). Evidences of ceremonial development are again lacking. It was the Guayabitoid people whom Columbus encountered when he discovered Trinidad and the Paria coast in 1498.

In the foregoing summary, we have taken up the ten Neo-Indian series roughly in the order in which they were discussed in the text, considering first the series which appear to have originated in western Venezuela, then the central Venezuelan series, and finally those native to the eastern part of the country. It may be noted that all of the western series, with the possible exception of the Tocuyanoid (2), are accompanied by some sort of ceremonial paraphernalia, such as figurines and amulets; and many of them also have elaborate forms of burial, such as shaft graves or urns. Several central series likewise occur in association with these kinds of remains, but the two eastern series, Saladoid (9) and Guayabitoid (10), lack them.

There is a similar distribution with respect to art, as the plates will illustrate. Only in western and central Venezuela, and in the segment of the Barrancoid series (5) which is presumed to have intruded from central into eastern Venezuela, is there a strong artistic development. This was impressed upon us when we selected the material for the plates; after finishing we found that we had chosen the largest number of artifacts from the western ceramic series, a considerable number from the series native to the central part of the country, but none at all from the two eastern series, Saladoid and Guayabitoid. We thereupon added several specimens from the Saladoid series (Pls. 46, B; 47), but even these must be regarded as basically central Venezuelan, for they reflect influence from the Barrancoid series. We conclude, therefore, that eastern Venezuela lacked an indigenous art form worthy of the name.

It will be remembered that the east coast of Venezuela lagged behind the rest of the country at the beginning of the Neo-Indian epoch, remaining on a Meso-Indian level of development for many centuries before Neo-Indians of the Saladoid series broke through the swamps of the Orinoco delta and the Paria coast. The backwardness of the eastern Neo-Indians in religion, burial, and art may be regarded as a repetition of the same phenomenon, of lag behind developments in the rest of the country. This second lag is particularly striking at the close of the Neo-Indian epoch, after the Saladoid series had degenerated into Guayabitoid.

What caused this lag in the east? In later Neo-Indian time, the region around the delta of the Orinoco River actually lay between two others with considerably greater ceremonial and artistic developments, west-central Venezuela on the one hand and the Greater Antilles on the other (Rouse, MS). We are inclined to attribute its relative backwardness to its remoteness. It was too far from the Intermediate area to be affected by the developments there which spread to western and central Venezuela, and it was too distant from Meso-America to be influenced by the latter, as the Greater Antilles may have been. It stagnated while western and central Venezuela were advancing in religion, burial, and art during the latter part of the Neo-Indian epoch.

Finally, it is of interest to note that two of the series, Dabajuroid (1) and Saladoid (9), are so broadly distributed on the coast and islands as to indicate extraordinary seafaring ability. The Dabajuroid and Saladoid people seem to have developed this ability in Venezuela's two great regions of sheltered water, Dabajuroid in the Lake of Maracaibo and the Gulf of Venezuela and Saladoid in the Gulfs of Cariaco and Paria, whence they expanded to the more open coasts and to the islands. One is tempted to correlate the two series with the two major groups of seafaring Indians in Columbus' time, the "Carib" and the "Arawak," but this would be a mistake. To judge from the distributions of the two, some Dabajuroid people must have spoken Cariban languages but others spoke Arawakan; and the same may have been true of the Saladoid people. As we have stated earlier (Chap. 2, D), such lack of correlation is to be expected; the Gothic style of architecture, for example, is not limited to French speakers, nor Chinese-style porcelain to the Chinese themselves.

Indo-Hispanic epoch. The Europeans first settled Cubagua and Margarita Islands, off the east coast of Venezuela, and subsequently expanded to the mainland, gradually taking over the coast, the mountains, and the Llanos from the Indian. Unlike the English in North America, they tended to assimilate the Indians, incorporating them in their towns and missions, intermarrying with them, and in general acculturating them to the European way of life. As a result, the Indian tribes of Venezuela have retained their identity only in the more remote areas—in the Guianan and Amazonian parts of the country, along the Colombian border, and in the Orinoco delta.

This process of acculturation is best documented archaeologically at the site of Nueva Cadiz on Cubagua Island. The excavations there have uncovered not only Spanish artifacts but also Indian pottery of styles native to various parts of the Caribbean area, which bear witness to the distances from which laborers were brought to the pearl fisheries. There is evidence that the Indian laborers soon abandoned these styles and developed a new, local form of pottery. This in turn survived with little modification throughout the Indo-Hispanic epoch and is still in existence as the folk pottery of the village of Manicuare on the Peninsula of Araya. It is, of course, only one of a series of contributions which the Indians have made to the modern culture of Venezuela.

PLATES

1 A

Plate 1. Kill sites of Taima Taima (A) and Muaco (B). Material was found in the mud around a spring to which men and animals were attracted.

1 B

above Plate 2. *Camp site of the Joboid series. Material is eroding out of the surface but is still in position.*

Plate 3. Typical stone artifacts of the Paleo-Indian epoch: A, tools, Manzanillo complex; B, chopping tool, Camare complex; C, D, blades, Las Lagunas complex; E, F, projectile points, El Jobo complex; G, projectile point, Las Casitas complex.

Plate 4. Incised fossil bones from Muaco: A, bone with intentional incision; B, detail of use of bone for an anvil; C, bone anvil.

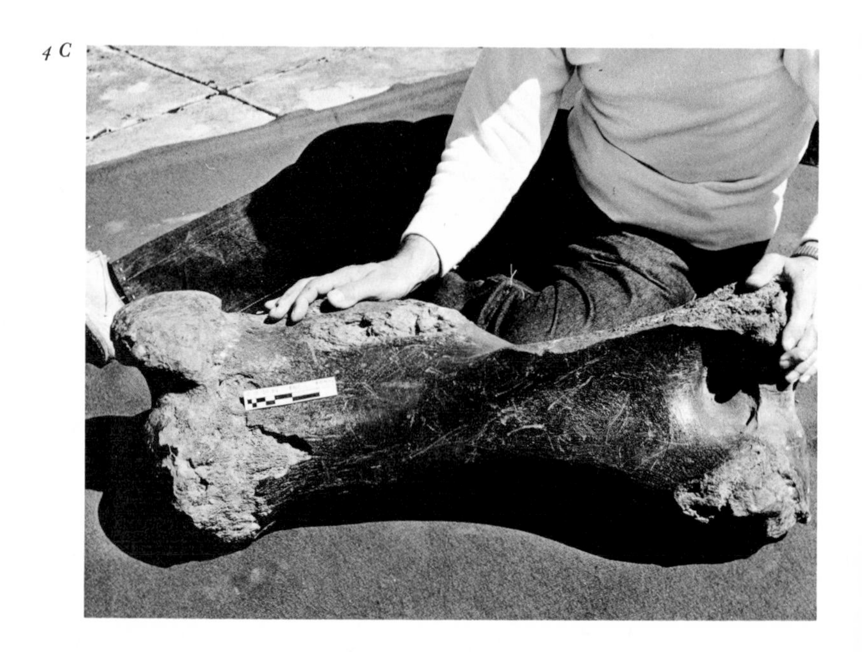

5 A

Plate 5. Shell heap and urn burial of the Meso-Indian epoch: A, excavation in the shell heap of Punta Gorda; B, urn containing a secondary burial, Rancho Peludo.

5 B

Plate 6. Chipped stone artifacts of the Canaima complex: A, projectile points; B, plano-convex scrapers; C, miscellaneous artifacts.

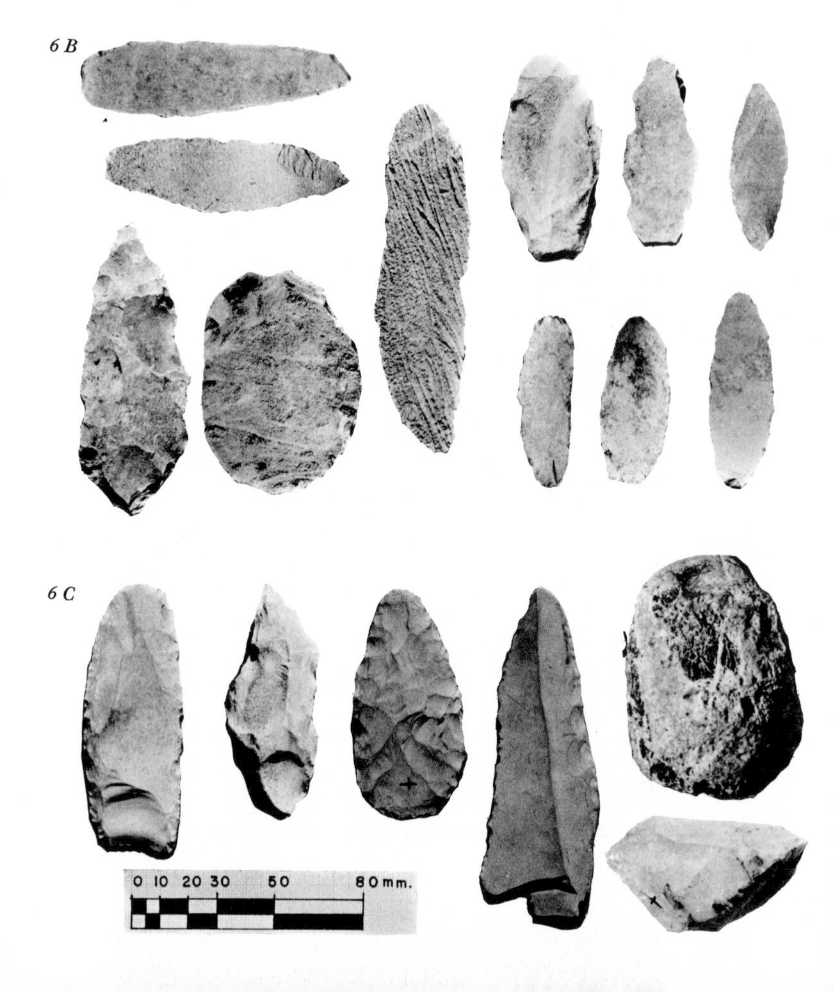

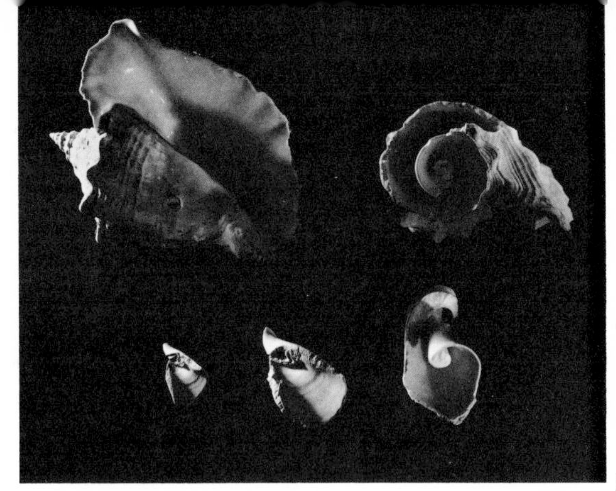

7 A

Plate 7. Manufacture of shell artifacts, Manicuare complex: A, stages in the manufacture of a shell gouge; B, stages in making a shell hammer and shell vessels; C, stages in the manufacture of a shell pendant.

7 B

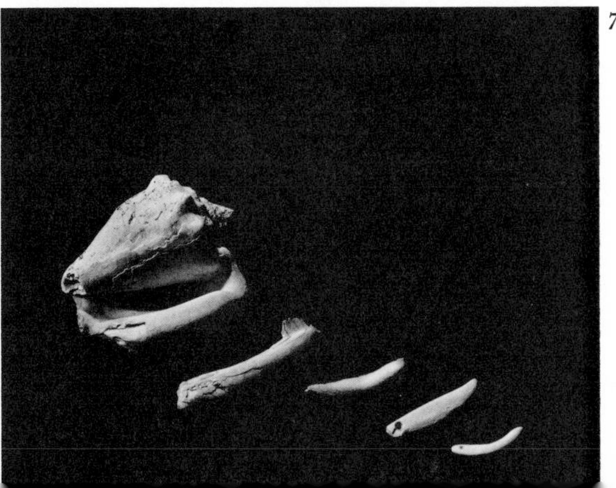

7 C

8 A *8 B*

Plate 8. Artifacts of the El Heneal (A, B) and Manicuare (C) complexes: A, hammerstones and pitted stone; B, red ocher, worked shell, and bone pin; C, petroglyph, milling stone, and hammerstones.

8 C

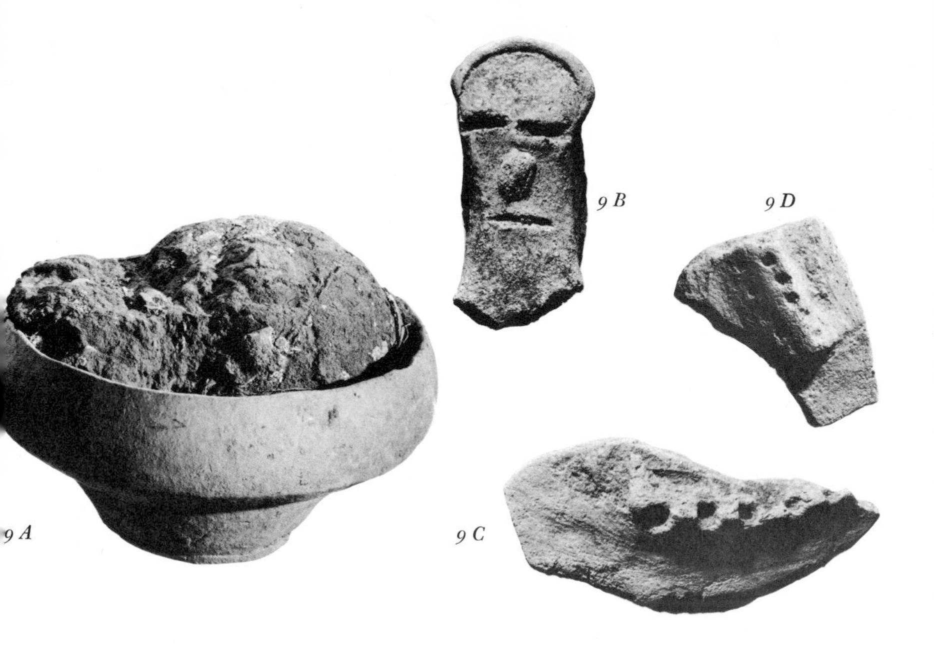

Plate 9. Pottery of the Rancho Peludo style: A, bowl with annular base, containing the secondary burial of a baby; B, human head; C, D, sherds decorated with appliqué work; E, olla with fabric-impressed base; F, plain bowl; G, plain jar.

10 A

Plate 10. Masonry and rock sites, Neo-Indian epoch: A, petroglyph, Quebrada Tusmare, Miranda; B, rock painting, Guajira Peninsula, Zulia; C, stone wall, Virigima, Carabobo;

10 B

10 C

10 D

Plate 10. D, mintoy, Mucuchies, Mérida; E, rock basin, Aguirre, Carabobo; F, rock mortars and a groove for honing axes, Ventuari, Amazonas.

10 E

10 F

11 A

Plate 11. Calzadas *and mound, Neo-Indian epoch: A, aerial view of the* calzada *of Paez, Barinas; B,* calzada *of Paez, Barinas; C, mound at Tocorón, Lake Valencia.*

11 B

11 C

12 A

Plate 12. Pottery of the Dabajuro style from Falcón: A, corrugated rim sherd; B, pottery lug painted black on white; C, black on white painted vessel, Sabaneta.

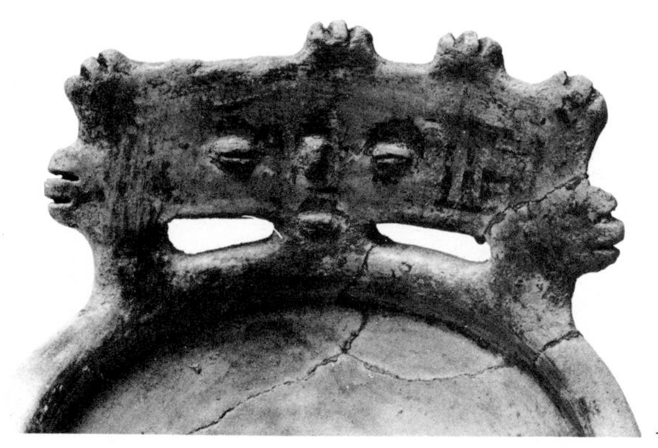

12 B

12 C

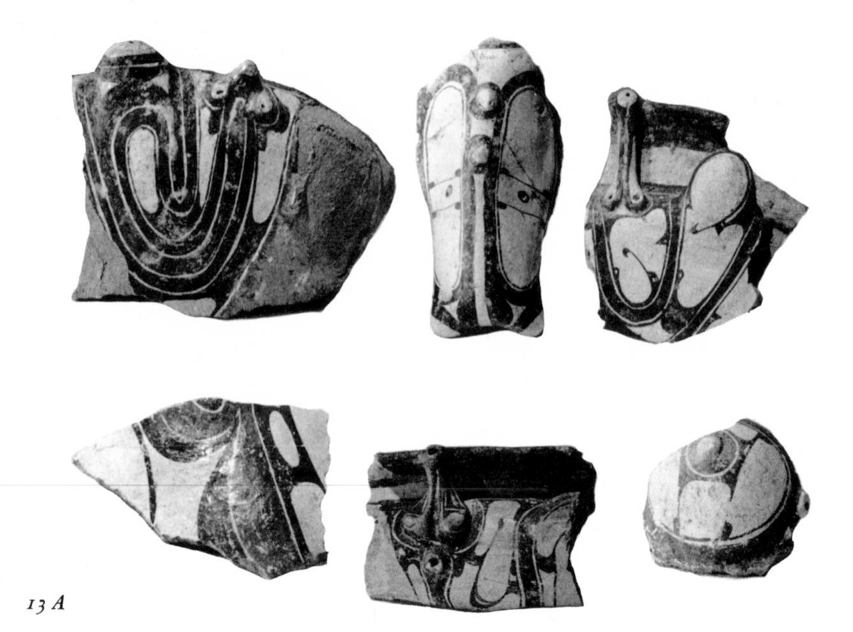

13 A

Plate 13. Pottery of the Tocuyano style from Tocuyano: A, sherds painted red and black on white; B, tetrapod vase, painted black on white.

13 B

Plate 14. Pottery of the Tocuyano style from Tocuyano: A, pottery lugs in the form of human faces, painted black on white; B, fragment of pot with hollow rim, painted red and black on white; C, bowl painted black on white.

15 A

Plate 15. Pottery of the Tocuyano style from Tocuyano: A, jar with face and serpent design; B, jar with geometric design.

15 B

16 A

Plate 16. Pottery of the Tocuyano style from Tocuyano: A, jar with serpent design; B, vessel painted red and black on white.

16 B

Plate 17. Tripod vessels of the Tierra de los Indios style, painted red and black on white, from the region of Quibor, Lara.

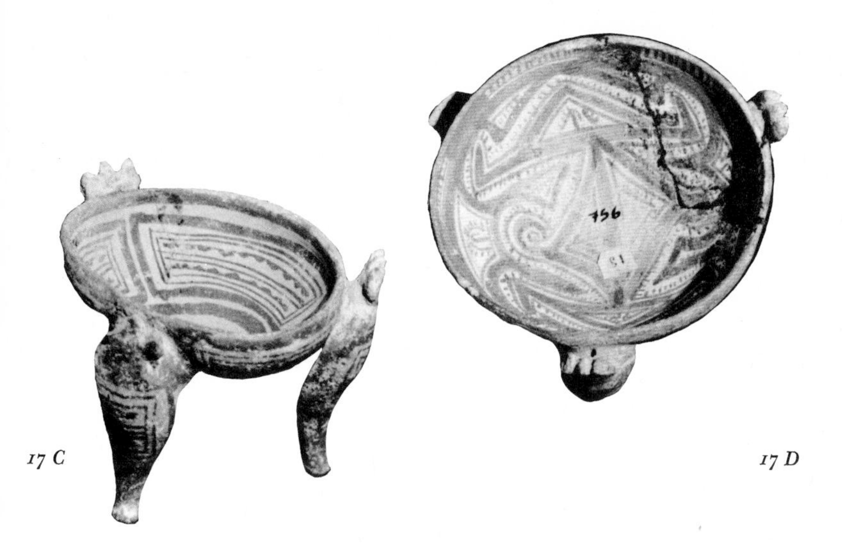

Plate 18. Pottery of the Tierra de los Indios style from Guadalupe, Lara: A, unpainted bowl; B, jar painted black on a plain background, pseudo-negative.

20 A

left Plate 19. *Jar with open annular base, of the Tierra de los Indios style, painted black on white, Guadalupe, Lara.*

right Plate 20. *Pottery of the Santa Ana style: A, B, tetrapod bowls, cave of Santo Domingo, Trujillo.*

20 B

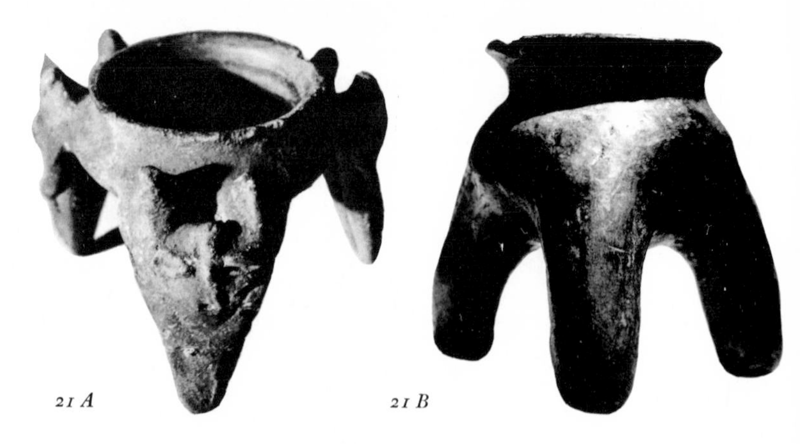

Plate 21. Pottery of various styles from Trujillo: A, tripod bowl of undetermined style, caves of Trujillo; B, incense vessel of undetermined style, caves of Trujillo; C, bowl of the Santa Ana style, cave of Santo Domingo; D, bowl with ring and leg base, Santa Ana style, painted black on white, cave of Santo Domingo.

21 C

21 D

22 *A*

Plate 22. Pottery of various styles, from Trujillo: A, vessel with ring and leg base, Santa Ana style, caves of Trujillo; B, tetrapod vessel, Santa Ana style, painted black on white, cave of Santo Domingo; C (left), *potsherd of the Betijoque style, painted black on white, Betijoque;* C (center), *bowl with ring and leg base, undetermined style, painted black on white, Tuname, Jajó;* C (right), *clay figurines, undetermined style, painted black on white, Niquitao, Boconó.*

22 *B*

22 *C*

23 A

23 B

23 C

left Plate 23. *Pottery of the Betijoque style from Betijoque: A, B, vessels with open annular bases, painted black on white; C, vessel with ring and leg base, painted black on white.*

right Plate 24. *Clay figurine of the Betijoque style, painted black on white, from Betijoque.*

left Plate 25. *Clay figurine of the Santa Ana style, painted black on white, from the cave of Santo Domingo, Trujillo.*

right Plate 26. *Clay figurine of undetermined style, front and back views, painted black on white, from Boconó, Trujillo.*

above Plate 27. *Clay figurine of undetermined style, area of Trujillo: unpainted, locality unknown.*

below Plate 28. *Stone figurines, from various localities, Trujillo.*

29 A

Plate 29. Ornamental stone work from various localities, Trujillo: A, carved amulets; B, bat-wing pendants.

29 B

30 A

Plate 30. Resin and metal figures, western Venezuela: A, figure of resin from Betijoque, Trujillo; B, figurine of gold alloy, found on the Peninsula of Guajira, Zulia.

30 B

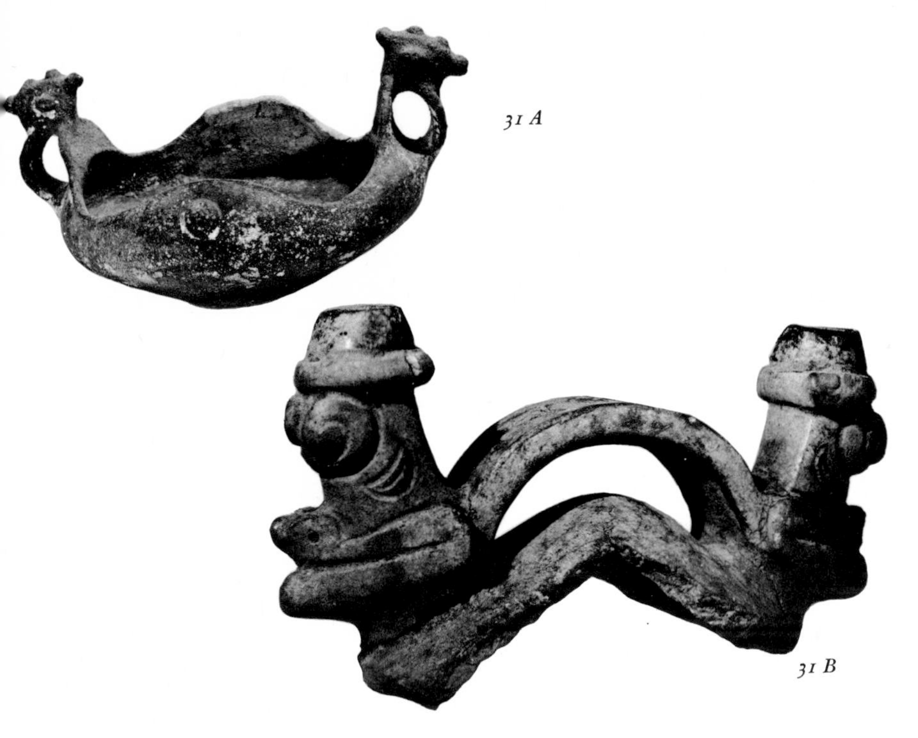

31 A

31 B

Plate 31. Pottery of the La Cabrera and Barrancas styles: A, bowl of the La Cabrera style found in the waters of Lake Valencia, Aragua; B, top of a double-spouted vessel, Barrancas style, Saladero, Monagas; C, bowl of the Barrancas style, Barrancas, Monagas.

31 C

32 A

Plate 32. Pottery of the Los Barrancos and Barrancas styles from Barrancas, Monagas: A, human face lug, Los Barrancos style; B, neck of a jar, Barrancas style.

32 B

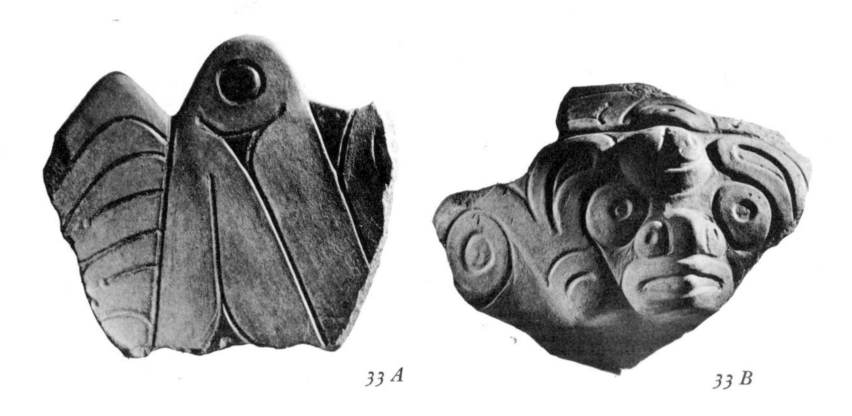

Plate 33. Pottery of the Los Barrancos style from Saladero, Monagas: A, C, incised sherds painted red in dull areas and highly polished in dark areas; B, part of a vessel, modeled and incised.

34 A

Plate 34. Pottery of the Los Barrancos style from Saladero, Monagas: A, B, modeled-incised lugs.

34 B

35 A

Plate 35. Clay pipes and pottery of the El Palito and Los Barrancos styles: A, clay pipes (left and right) *and pottery lugs* (center), *El Palito, Carabobo; B, vessel and lug, Los Barrancos style, Saladero, Monagas.*

35 B

36 A

left Plate 36. *A, stone pestle, El Palito style, Aserradero, Carabobo; B, clay pipe, La Cabrera style, Peninsula of La Cabrera, Aragua.*

right Plate 37. *Clay figurine of the Los Barrancos style, from Barrancas, Monagas.*

36 B

38 A

38 B

Plate 38. Bone flute, La Cabrera style and clay stamps from the Llanos: A, bone flute from the Valencia basin; B, cylindrical clay stamps.

39 A

39 B

39 C

Plate 39. Pottery of the Valencia style: A, bowl, Valencia basin; B, D, bowls with open annular bases, Peninsula of La Cabrera, Aragua; C, E, bottles, Valencia basin.

39 D

39 E

40 A

40 B

Plate 40. Pottery of the Valencia style from the Valencia basin: A, C, jars decorated with human faces; B, bowl.

Plate 41. Clay figurine of the Valencia style, from the Valencia basin.

40 C

Plate 42. Clay figurine of the Valencia style, from the Valencia basin.

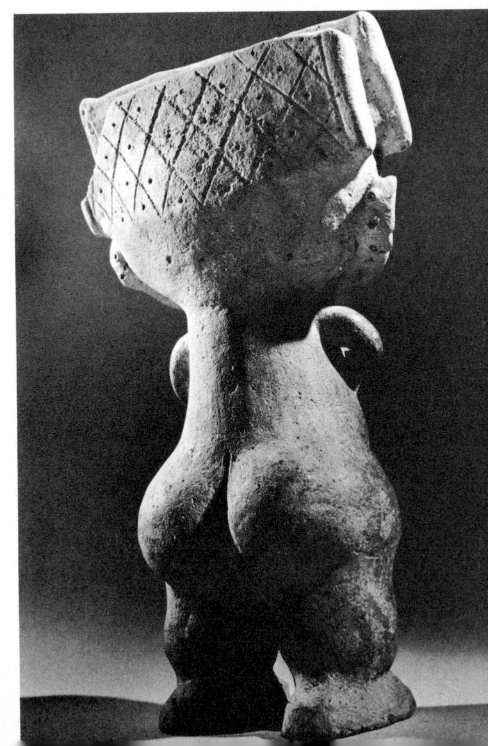

Plate 43. Clay figurine of the Valencia style, from the Peninsula of La Cabrera, Aragua.

Plate 44. Clay figurines of the Valencia style, from the Valencia basin.

above Plate 45. *Clay pipe of the Valencia style, from the Peninsula of La Cabrera, Aragua.*

below Plate 46. *Shell pendant, central Venezuela, and pottery of the El Agua style: A, shell pendant, Los Teques, Miranda; B, pottery lug, Güire Güire, Nueva Esparta.*

46 A

46 B

47 *A-D*

Plate 47. Pottery of the El Mayal style, from La Cucaracha, Carúpano, Sucre: A–D, white-on-red painted sherds; E, F, crosshatch-incised sherds;

47 *E*

47 *F*

47 G

G–J, modeled-incised pottery.

47 H

47 I

47 J

48 A

left Plate 48. *Ruins of Nueva Cadiz: A, aerial view; B, remnants of the walls of houses.*

right Plate 49. *Burial at Nueva Cadiz.*

48 B

50 A

Plate 50. Pottery from Nueva Cadiz: A, salad bowl; B, plate.

50 B

51 A

Plate 51. Pottery from Nueva Cadiz: A, olive jar; **B**, *fragment of an olive jar.*

51 B

52 A

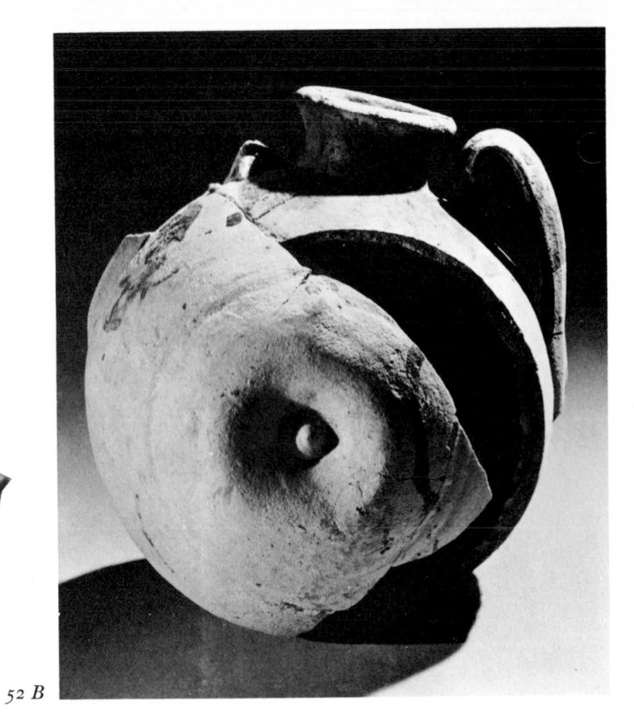

52 B

Plate 52. Pottery from Nueva Cadiz: A, potsherd engraved with the date of manufacture; B, C, olive jars.

52 C

53 A

Plate 53. Clay and lead stamps from Nueva Cadiz: A, clay stamp with royal mark of Ferdinand and Isabela, for sealing letters; B, lead stamp with religious motif, probably for making designs on cloth.

53 B

54 A

54 B

Plate 54. Stone sculptures from Nueva Cadiz: A, gargoyle with a water trough running down its back; B, stone column, resting on an accumulation of shells from the pearl fisheries; C, part of a Spanish coat of arms.

54 C

55 *A*

Plate 55. Stone sculptures from Nueva Cadiz: A, gargoyle drilled with a hole for the water to come out of the mouth (the bearded face of a Spaniard may be seen on the side); B, coat of arms.

55 *B*

Appendix.

VENEZUELAN RADIOCARBON DATES

The following list contains all known radiocarbon dates for Venezuela, including 52 which appear to be valid and 5 which are obviously incorrect. A series of comments is appended to explain the incorrect dates.

The dates are listed in order of sample letters and numbers. The letters refer to the laboratories where the analyses were done: M, University of Michigan; O, Humble Oil Company; P, University of Pennsylvania; and Y, Yale University. Since these laboratories assign numbers in order of receipt of the samples, a lower number indicates that a sample was catalogued and (in most cases) analyzed earlier than a sample with a higher number. In other words, a sample with a lower number did not benefit from the refinements of the technique applied to the samples with higher numbers.

The description of each sample is limited to the site from which it came, the complex or style with which it was associated, and the period of that style in our relative chronology. Information concerning the nature of the sample and further details about its associations may be obtained by consulting the official date lists of the various laboratories, as published in *Science* before 1959, and in *Radiocarbon* (Flint and Deevey, 1959–62).

The dates themselves are given in two forms: B.P., which means "before the present"; and B.C. or A.D., in terms of our Christian calendar. The B.P. dates are the definitive figures, as published in the official date lists and used in our technical monograph (Cruxent and Rouse, 1958–59, 1961). The Christian calendar dates are modifications of the original figures, intended to make the dates more comprehensible to the readers of this volume. They are not, therefore, comparable to the official figures and should not be quoted as such.

Before converting each B.P. date into B.C. or A.D., we have increased it by 3 per cent in order to correct for the recent redetermination of the half-life of carbon 14 by the U. S. Bureau of Standards. This correction is tentative, since work is still being done on the half-life, but we have made it anyway in order to give the reader a better idea of the actual magnitudes of the dates, in accordance with the advice of the 1962 radiocarbon conference at Cambridge, England (Godwin, 1962).

After making the correction, we converted into B.C. or A.D. by subtracting 1950 from the B.P. date. This, too, is a departure from previous practice, which was to subtract the year in which analysis was done; and conforms to a recent recommendation by radiocarbon authorities (Flint and Deevey, 1959–62, vol. 4, p. v). Strictly speaking, the 1950 figure should be applied only to dates obtained since 1958, when oxalic acid was adopted as a radiocarbon standard. However, the use of this figure for the earlier dates can cause no more than a five-year error, which is insignificant relative to the errors inherent in the dating process itself, and so it has seemed better to apply the 1950 figure throughout for the sake of consistency.

All dates have been rounded off to zero or, in a few cases, to five years. This is done to emphasize the approximate nature of the dates. Each represents a statistical probability rather than the time when a given event actually took place.

Radiocarbon Dates

Sample no.	*Site*	*Complex or style*	*Period*	*Date B.P.*	*Christian date*
M-257	Tocuyano	Tocuyano	II	2180 ± 300	295 B.C.
M-1068	Muaco	El Jobo (?)	–	14,300 ± 500	12,780 B.C.
O-999	Muaco	El Jobo (?)	–	16,375 ± 400	14,920 B.C.
P-160	AM-2, Nericagua	Nericagua	III	1189 ± 93	725 A.D.
P-161	AM-2, Nericagua	Nericagua	III	1159 ± 122	760 A.D.
P-162	AM-4, Martínez	Nericagua	IV	619 ± 103	1320 A.D.
P-163	AM-4, Martínez	Nericagua	IV	544 ± 113	1390 A.D.
P-164	AM-7, Canaraven	Nericagua	IV	585 ± 93	1350 A.D.
P-165	AM-7, Canaraven	Nericagua	IV	654 ± 93	1280 A.D.
P-166	AM-8, Morillo	Nericagua	IV	843 ± 96	1080 A.D.
P-169	AM-9, Minisia Vieja	Nericagua	IV	850 ± 95	1070 A.D.
P-261	AM-4, Martínez	Nericagua	III	1263 ± 54	650 A.D.
P-262	AM-4, Martínez	Nericagua	III	1032 ± 54	890 A.D.
Y-38–39	Saladero	Guarguapo	V	300 ± 50	1640 A.D.
Y-40	Saladero	Barrancas	II	2850 ± 120	985 B.C.
Y-41	Saladero	Barrancas	II	6250 ± 380	(See note 1 below)
Y-42	Saladero	Saladero	II	2870 ± 130	1010 B.C.
Y-43	Saladero	Saladero	II	2700 ± 130	830 B.C.
Y-44	Saladero	Saladero	II	2570 ± 130	700 B.C.
Y-290	Irapa	Irapa	III	1580 ± 40	325 A.D.
Y-294	Saladero	Barrancas	II	2800 ± 150	930 B.C.
Y-295	La Aduana	Manicuare	I	3570 ± 130	1730 B.C.
Y-296g	La Aduana	Manicuare	I	3050 ± 80	1190 B.C.
Y-297	El Mayal 2	El Mayal	II	1795 ± 80	100 A.D.
Y-298	El Morro	El Morro	IV	715 ± 70	1210 A.D.
Y-299	Calle de la Marina	El Morro	V	290 ± 70	1650 A.D.
Y-300	El Mayal 1	Chuare	III	1355 ± 80	550 A.D.
Y-316	Saladero	Barrancas	II	2820 ± 80	955 B.C.
Y-438	El Jobo	El Jobo	–	–	(See note 2 below)
Y-439	El Jobo	El Jobo	–	–	(See note 2 below)
Y-454	Mirinday	Mirinday	IV	580 ± 50	1350 A.D.
Y-455	El Heneal	El Heneal	I	3400 ± 120	1550 B.C.
Y-456	Pedro García	Pedro García	I	2450 ± 90	570 B.C.
Y-457	Cerro Machado	Cerro Machado	II	1930 ± 70	40 B.C.
Y-497	Punta Gorda	Cubagua	I	4150 ± 80	2325 B.C.
Y-499	Los Barrancos	Los Barrancos	III	1370 ± 90	510 A.D.
Y-578	Rancho Peludo	Rancho Peludo	I	4630 ± 150	2820 B.C.
Y-579	Aserradero	El Palito	II	1640 ± 120	260 A.D.
Y-580	Aserradero	El Palito	II	1615 ± 120	290 A.D.
Y-630	La Mata	Valencia	III	1000 ± 70	920 A.D.
Y-631	La Mata	Valencia	III	980 ± 110	940 A.D.
Y-632	La Mata	Valencia	III	1000 ± 100	920 A.D.
Y-852	Cerro Iguanas	El Heneal	I	5550 ± 100	3770 B.C.
Y-853	Cerro Iguanas	El Heneal	I	5190 ± 120	3400 B.C.

Radiocarbon Dates (*Continued*)

Sample no.	*Site*	*Complex or style*	*Period*	*Date B.P.*	*Christian date*
Y-854	Cerro Iguanas	El Heneal	I	5580 ± 160	3800 B.C.
Y-855	La Pitía	Hokomo	II	1880 ± 110	10 B.C.
Y-1108-I	Rancho Peludo	Rancho Peludo	II	2325 ± 80	445 B.C.
Y-1108-II	Rancho Peludo	Rancho Peludo	II	2680 ± 90	810 B.C.
Y-1108-III	Rancho Peludo	Rancho Peludo	II	6190 ± 90	(See note 3 below)
Y-1108-IV	Rancho Peludo	Manzanillo (?)	I	13,915 ± 200	12,380 B.C.
Y-1109	Rancho Peludo	Rancho Peludo	I	3750 ± 80	1910 B.C.
Y-1110	Rancho Peludo	Rancho Peludo	I	3810 ± 85	1970 B.C.
Y-1111	Amacuro	Guayabita	IV	690 ± 70	1240 A.D.
Y-1112	Cabrantica	Irapa	III	1320 ± 95	570 A.D.
Y-1113	Punta de Piedras	Irapa	II	1680 ± 85	220 A.D.
Y-1199	Taima Taima	Taima Taima	–	>41,000	(See note 4 below)
Y-1230	La Cucaracha	El Mayal	II	1600 ± 100	300 A.D.
Y-1231	Río Guapo	Río Guapo	II	1630 ± 100	270 A.D.

1. Sample Y-41, from Saladero, yielded an impossibly old date. It had been prepared twice, once for solid-carbon counting and then for the new gaseous method, and apparently lost radioactivity in the process.

2. Samples Y-438 and Y-439, from El Jobo, yielded modern dates. Both came from the surface and must be the result of fires set by the present inhabitants of the site.

3. Sample Y-1108-III, from Rancho Peludo, is believed to be a mixture of charcoal from two successive occupations of the site, dated by samples Y-1108-IV and Y-1108-II respectively. If so, its date must be disregarded (Rouse and Cruxent, 1963).

4. Sample Y-1199, from Taima Taima, contained too little radioactivity to be measured. This raised the question whether it actually was charcoal, as had been thought, or whether it might be some inert substance, such as pitch or coal. It looked shiny like coal, we found that there were coal deposits in the vicinity, these contained sulphur, and analysis of the sample revealed that it has a similar proportion of sulphur. Therefore, sample Y-1199 is considered to be coal and not a true measure of the age of the site.

BIBLIOGRAPHY

Alegría, Ricardo E., 1955. La tradición cultural arcaica antillana. In *Miscelanea de Estudios dedicados a Fernando Ortiz,* vol. 1, pp. 43–62. La Habana: Sociedad Económica de Amigos del Pais.

Alvarado, Lisandro, 1945. *Datos etnográficos de Venezuela.* Caracas: Biblioteca Venezolana de Cultura, Colección "Viajes y Naturaleza."

Andel, Tj. van, and H. Postma, 1954. Recent Sediments of the Gulf of Paria: Reports of the Orinoco Shelf Expedition, Volume 1. *Verhandelingen der Koninklijke Nederlandse Akademie van Wetenschappen, afd. Naturkunde,* Amsterdam, eerste reeks, *20,* no. 5.

Avelyra A. de Anda, Luis, 1955. El segundo mamut fósil de Santa Isabel Iztapan, México, y artifactos asociados. *Instituto Nacional de Antropología e Historia, Dirección de Prehistoria, Publicaciones,* no. 1. México: Instituto Nacional de Antropología e Historia.

Bennett, Wendell C., 1937. Excavations at La Mata, Maracay, Venezuela. *Anthropological Papers of the American Museum of Natural History, 36,* pt. 2.

Bennett, Wendell C., and Junius Bird, 1960. Andean Culture History. Second and revised edition. *American Museum of Natural History, Handbook Series,* no. 15.

Booy, Theodoor de, 1916. Notes on the Archeology of Margarita Island, Venezuela. *Contributions from the Museum of the American Indian, Heye Foundation, 2,* no. 5.

Braidwood, Robert J., and Gordon R. Willey, editors, 1962. Courses toward Urban Life; Archeological Considerations of Some Cultural Alternates. *Viking Fund Publications in Anthropology,* no. 32.

Briceño Iragorry, M., 1928. *Ornamentos fúnebres de los aborígenes del occidente de Venezuela.* Caracas.

Childe, V. Gordon, 1956. *Piecing Together the Past: the Interpretation of Archaeological Data.* London: Routlege and Kegan Paul.

Coe, Michael D., 1962. Costa Rican Archaeology and Mesoamerica. *Southwestern Journal of Anthropology, 18,* no. 2, pp. 170–83.

Comas, Juan, 1959. L'anthropologie américaine et le diffusionisme de P. Laviosa Zambotti. *Trabalhos de Antropologia e Etnologia da Sociedade Portugesa de Antropologia e Etnologia e do Centro de Estudos de Etnologia Peninsular, 17,* nos. 1–4, pp. 43–52.

Cruxent, José M., 1951. Venezuela: a Strategic Center for Caribbean Archeology. In *The Caribbean at Mid-Century,* edited by A. Curtis Wilgus, pp. 149–56. Gainesville: University of Florida Press.

——— 1952. Notes on Venezuelan Archeology. In *Indian Tribes of Aboriginal America: Selected Papers of the XXIXth International Congress of Americanists,* edited by Sol Tax, pp. 280–94. Chicago: University of Chicago Press.

——— 1955. Nueva Cadiz, testimonio de piedras. *El Farol,* Caracas, año 17, no. 160, pp. 2–5.

——— 1957. Noticia sobre los trabajos arqueológicos realizados durante la expedición de la Sociedad Venezolana de Ciencias Naturales al Río Guasare (Zulia). *Boletín de la Sociedad Venezolana de Ciencias Naturales, 18,* no. 88, pp. 122–24.

——— 1961. Huesos quemados en el yacimiento prehistórico Muaco, Edo. Falcón. *Instituto Venezolano de Investigaciones Científicas, Departamento de Antropología, Boletín Informativo,* no. 2, pp. 20–21.

——— 1962. Artifacts of Paleo-Indian Type, Maracaibo, Zulia, Venezuela. *American Antiquity, 27,* no. 4, pp. 576–79.

——— MS. Pinturas rupestres en la Goagira. Trabajo presentado a la XI Convención Anual de la Asociación Venezolana para el Avance de la Ciencia. Manuscript in the Instituto Venezolano de Investigaciones Científicas, Caracas.

Cruxent, J. M., and M. Rolando, 1961. Tipologia morfológica de tres piezas de cerámica; Nueva Cadiz, Isla de Cubagua. *Instituto Venezolano de Investigaciones Científicas, Departamento de Antropología, Boletín Informativo,* no. 2, pp. 7–19.

Cruxent, J. M., and Irving Rouse, 1958–59. An Archeological Chronology of Venezuela. *Pan American Union, Social Science Monographs,* no. 6 (2 vols.).

——— 1959. Venezuela and its Relationships with Neighboring Areas. In *Actas del XXXIII Congreso Internacional de Americanistas, San José, 20–27 Julio 1958,* tomo 1, pp. 173–83. San José, C. R.: Lehmann.

——— 1961. Una cronología arqueológica de Venezuela. *Unión Pan Americana, Estudios Monográficos,* no. 4 (2 vols.).

De Laet, Sigfried J., 1957. *Archaeology and Its Problems.* London: Phoenix House Ltd.

Du Rhy, C. J., and H. R. van Heekeren, 1960. Studies in the Archaeology of the Netherlands Antilles: I–II. *Uitgaven van de "Natuurwetenschappelijke Werkgroep Nederlandse Antillen,"* no. 10. Willemstad: Boekhandel Salas.

Dupouy, Walter, 1956. Dos piezas de tipo Paleolítico de la Gran Sabana, Venezuela. *Boletín del Museo de Ciencias Naturales,* Caracas, *2–3,* pp. 95–102.

——— 1960. Tres puntas líticas de tipo Paleo-Indio de la Paragua, Estada Bolívar, Venezuela. *Boletín del Museo de Ciencias Naturales,* Caracas, *5–6,* pp. 7–14.

Ernst, Adolfo, 1886. *La exposición nacional de Venezuela en 1883.* Caracas.

Evans, Clifford, and Betty J. Meggers, 1960. Archeological Investigations in British Guiana. *Bureau of American Ethnology, Bulletin* no. 177.

Evans, Clifford; Betty J. Meggers; and José M. Cruxent, 1959. Preliminary Results of Archeological Investigations along the Orinoco and Ventuari Rivers, Venezuela. In *Actas del XXXIII Congreso Internacional de Americanistas, San José, 20–27 Julio 1958,* tomo 2, pp. 359–69. San José, C. R.: Lehmann.

Febres Cordero, Tulio, 1920. *Décadas de la historia de Mérida.* Mérida: Tipografía "El Lápiz."

Flint, Richard F., 1957. *Glacial and Pleistocene Geology.* New York: John Wiley and Sons, Inc.

Flint, Richard F., and Edward S. Deevey, editors, 1959–62. Radiocarbon (Supplement, *American Journal of Science*), vols. 1–4.

Ford, James Alfred, 1949. Cultural Dating of Prehistoric Sites in Virú Valley, Peru. In "Surface Survey of the Virú Valley, Peru," *Anthropological Papers of the American Museum of Natural History, 43,* pt. 1, pp. 29–89.

Fuchs, Helmuth, 1960. Noticia sobre el viaje realizado al sitio arqueológico Capacho II, Edo. Táchira. *Folia Antropológica,* Caracas, no. 1, pp. 73–78.

Gallagher, Patrick, 1962. La Pitía. *El Farol,* Caracas, año 24, Julio/Agosto, pp. 6–14.

Gil Fortoul, José, 1943. *Historia constitucional de Venezuela.* Tercera edición revisada. 3 vols. Caracas: Editorial "Las Novedades."

Gines, Hno., Fr. Cayetano de Carrocera, J. M. Cruxent, and Jesús M. Rísquez, 1946. Manicuare: trabajo presentado a la IV Asamblea Panamericana de Geografía e Historia. *Memorias de la Sociedad de Ciencias Naturales La Salle,* Caracas, no. 16, pp. 157–200.

Godwin, L. E., 1962. Half-life of Radiocarbon. *Nature, 195,* no. 4845, p. 984.

González, Alberto Rex, 1952. Antiguo horizonte precerámico en las Sierras Centrales de Argentina. *Runa: Archivo para las Ciencias del Hombre,* Buenos Aires, *5,* pp. 110–33.

Harrington, M. R., 1933. Gypsum Cave, Nevada. *Southwest Museum Papers,* no. 8.

Haury, Emil W., and Julio César Cubillos, 1953. Investigaciones arqueológicas en la sabana de Bogotá, Colombia (cultura Chibcha). *University of Arizona Bulletin, 24,* no. 2.

Howard, George D., 1943. Excavations at Ronquín, Venezuela. *Yale University Publications in Anthropology,* no. 28.

——— 1947. Prehistoric Ceramic Styles of Lowland South America, Their Distribution and History. *Yale University Publications in Anthropology,* no. 37.

Jahn, Alfredo, 1927. *Los aborígenes des occidente de Venezuela.* Caracas: Librería y Tipografía del Comercio.

——— 1931. *El deshielo de la Sierra Nevada de Mérida y sus causas.* Caracas.

Kidder, Alfred, II, 1944. Archaeology of Northwestern Venezuela. *Papers of the Peabody Museum of American Archaeology and Ethnology, Harvard University, 26,* no. 1.

Libby, Willard F., 1955. *Radiocarbon Dating.* Chicago: University of Chicago Press.

Linné, S., 1925. The Technique of South American Ceramics. *Göteborgs Kungl. Vetenskapoch Vitterhets-Samhälles Handlingar, fjärde följden, 29,* no. 5.

Lothrop, Samuel K., 1942. Coclé: an Archaeological Study of Central Panama; Part II, Pottery of Sitio Conté and Other Archaeological Sites. *Memoirs of the Peabody Museum of Archaeology and Ethnology, Harvard University,* no. 8.

MacNeish, Richard Stockton, 1962. *Second Annual Report of the Tehuacan Archaeological Botanical Project.* Andover, Mass.: Robert S. Peabody Foundation for Archaeology.

Marcano, Gaspar, 1889. Ethnographie précolombienne du Venezuela, valles d'Aragua et de Caracas. *Mémoires de la Société d'Anthropologie de Paris, 4,* pp. 1–86.

Meggers, Betty J., and Clifford Evans, 1961. An Experimental

Formulation of Horizon Styles in the Tropical Forest Area of South America. In *Essays in Pre-Columbian Art and Archaeology,* by Samuel K. Lothrop and others, pp. 372–88. Cambridge: Harvard University Press.

Morison, Samuel Eliot, 1942. *Admiral of the Ocean Sea: a Life of Christopher Columbus.* 2 vols. Boston: Little, Brown and Co.

Morón, Guillermo, 1954. Los orígenes históricos de Venezuela: introducción al siglo XVI. Madrid: Consejo Superior de Investigaciones Científicas, Instituto "Gonzalo Fernández de Oviedo."

Oramas, Luis R., 1917. Apuntes sobre arqueología venezolana. *Proceedings of the Second Pan American Scientific Congress,* Washington, *1,* pp. 138–45.

Osgood, Cornelius, 1943. Excavations at Tocorón, Venezuela. *Yale University Publications in Anthropology,* no. 29.

Osgood, Cornelius, and George D. Howard, 1943. An Archeological Survey of Venezuela. *Yale University Publications in Anthropology,* no. 27.

Otte, Enrique, 1961. *Cedulario de la monarquia española relativo a la isla de Cubagua (1523–1550).* 2 vols. Caracas: Imprenta y Editorial Maestre.

Petrullo, Vincenzo, 1939. Archeology of Arauquín. *Bureau of American Ethnology, Bulletin* no. 123, pp. 291–95.

Petzall, Wolf, MS. Informe sobre la geología de las estaciones arqueológicas en la región de El Jobo, Falcón, Venezuela. Manuscript in the Instituto Venezuelano de Investigaciones Científicas, Caracas.

Reichel-Dolmatoff, Gerardo, 1954. A Preliminary Study of Space and Time Perspective in Northern Colombia. *American Antiquity, 19,* no. 4, pp. 352–66.

——— 1957. Momíl: a Formative Sequence from the Sinú Valley, Colombia. *American Antiquity, 22,* no. 3, pp. 226–34.

——— 1961. Puerto Hormiga: un complejo prehistórico marginal de Colombia (nota preliminar). *Revista Colombiana de Antropología, 10,* pp. 349–54.

Requena, Antonio, 1947. Figuración en alfarería antropomorfa precolombina venezolano de aparatos de deformación craneana artificial e intencional. *Acta Venezolana, 2,* no. 1–4, pp. 24–35.

Requena, Rafael, 1932. *Vestigios de la Atlántida.* Caracas: Tipografía Americana.

Riley, Carroll L., and Charles W. Olvey, 1960. Additional Ronquín Sites in the Middle Orinoco Valley. *American Antiquity, 25,* no. 4, pp. 579–9.

Rouse, Irving, 1951. Areas and Periods of Culture in the Greater Antilles. *Southwestern Journal of Anthropology, 7,* no. 3, pp. 248–65.

——— 1953a. The Circum-Caribbean Theory, an Archeological Test. *American Anthropologist, 55,* no. 2, pp. 188–200.

——— 1953b. Indian Sites in Trinidad. In "On the Excavation of a Shell Mound at Palo Seco, Trinidad, B.W.I." by J. A. Bullbrook. *Yale University Publications in Anthropology,* no. 50, pp. 94–111.

——— 1954. Reply to Stern's Note. *American Anthropologist, 56,* no. 1, pp. 107–08.

——— 1955. On the Correlation of Phases of Culture. *American Anthropologist, 57,* no. 4, pp. 713–22.

——— 1960. The Entry of Man into the West Indies. *Yale University Publications in Anthropology,* no. 61.

——— MS. Caribbean Area. Manuscript to be published in *Prehistoric Man in the New World,* edited by Jesse D. Jennings. Chicago: University of Chicago Press.

Rouse, Irving, Ricardo E. Alegría, and Minze Stuiver, MS. Recent Radiocarbon Dates for the West Indies. Manuscript in the Department of Anthropology, Yale University.

Rouse, Irving, and J. M. Cruxent, 1957. Further Comment on the Finds at El Jobo, Venezuela. *American Antiquity, 22,* no. 4, p. 412.

——— 1963. Some Recent Radiocarbon Dates for Western Venezuela. *American Antiquity, 28,* no. 4, pp. 537–40.

Rouse, Irving, José M. Cruxent, and Erika Wagner, MS. New Data on the Chronology of Venezuela. Manuscript in the Department of Anthropology, Yale University.

Royo y Gómez, José, 1956. Cuaternario en Venezuela. In "Léxico estrátigrafico de Venezuela," *Ministerio de Minas e Hidrocarburos Dirección de Geología, Boletín de Geología, Publicación Especial,* Caracas, no. 1, pp. 199–209.

——— 1960a. Características paleontológicas y geológicas del yacimiento de vertebratas de Muaco, Estado Falcón, con industria lítica humana. In "Memoria del III Congreso Geológico Venezolano," tomo 2; *Boletín de Geología, Publicación Especial,* Caracas, no. 3, pp. 501–05.

——— 1960b. Pleistocene Vertebrates from the Muaco Deposit. Society of Vertebrate Paleontology, *News Bulletin,* no. 58, pp. 31–32.

——— 1960c. El yacimiento de vertebrados pleistocenos de Muaco, Estado Falcón, Venezuela, con industria lítica humana. *Report of the International Geological Congress, XXI Session, Nor-*

den, pt. 4, pp. 154–57. Copenhagen: Berlingske Bogtrykkeri.

Sauer, Carl O., 1952. *Agricultural Origins and Dispersals.* New York: American Geographical Society.

Schobinger, Juan, 1959. Esquema de la prehistoria argentina. *Ampurias: Revista de Prehistoria, Arqueología y Etnología,* Barcelona, *21,* pp. 29–67.

Sellards, E. H., 1960. Some Early Stone Artifact Developments in North America. *Southwestern Journal of Anthropology, 16,* no. 2, pp. 160–73.

Simon Velásquez, Justo, 1956. Petroleo y perlas en Cubagua. *Revista Shell,* Caracas, año 5, no. 18, pp. 45–52.

Smith, Watson, 1962. Schools, Pots, and Potters. *American Anthropologist, 64,* no. 6, pp. 1165–78.

Société d'Histoire de la Martinique, 1963. *Premier Congrès International d'Etudes des Civilisations Précolombiennes des Petites Antilles, Fort-de-France, 3–7 Juillet 1961, Compte-rendu intégral des communications et débats,* Fascicule 1. Fort-de-France.

Vila, Pablo, 1960. *Geografía de Venezuela: vol. 1, El territorio nacional y su ambiente físico.* Caracas: Ministerio de Educación.

Wilbert, Johannes, 1956. Rasgos culturales circumcaribes entre Los Warrau y sus inferencias. *Memorias de la Sociedad de Ciencias Naturales La Salle,* Caracas, *16,* no. 45, pp. 237–57.

Willey, Gordon R., 1945. Horizon Styles and Pottery Traditions in Peruvian Archaeology. *American Antiquity, 11,* no. 1, pp. 49–56.

——— 1958. Estimated Correlations and Dating of South and Central American Culture Sequences. *American Antiquity, 23,* no. 4, pp. 353–78.

——— 1960a. Historical Patterns and Evolution in Native New World Cultures. In *Evolution after Darwin,* edited by Sol Tax, vol. 2, pp. 111–41. Chicago: University of Chicago Press.

——— 1960b. New World Prehistory. *Science, 131,* no. 3393, pp. 73–86.

Willey, Gordon R., and Philip Phillips, 1958. *Method and Theory in American Archaeology.* Chicago: University of Chicago Press.

Wing, Elisabeth S., 1961. Animal Remains Excavated at the Spanish Site of Nueva Cadiz on Cubagua Island, Venezuela. *Niewe West-Indische Gids, 41,* no. 2, pp. 162–65.

Wormington, H. M., 1957. Ancient Man in North America. Fourth edition. *Denver Museum of Natural History, Popular Series,* no. 4.

Zeuner, Frederick E., 1959. *The Pleistocene Period: Its Climate, Chronology and Faunal Successions.* London: Hutchison and Co. Ltd.

INDEX